Darin Sargent is a treasure. For over thirty-five years I've had a front row friendship view as Darin grew beyond challenges and instead turned them into his destiny. In *Battle the Beast: Defeating the Lions That Oppose Your Destiny* he challenges us to "be intentional in addressing our inner world." Darin boldly and scripturally confronts and unveils the twelve "lions" which can limit our effectiveness in the kingdom of God. He gives us instruction not just how to identify these enemies but how we can overcome them. Thank you, Darin, for this reminder: "Your life is too valuable not to leave a lasting imprint and effect on your family, community, and the world at large!"

—**Tim Gaddy**, Senior Pastor, New Life Church
Cabot, Arkansas

Darin Sargent writes like he speaks and lives: brilliant communicator, outrageous fun, self-deprecating humor, whimsical witticism, all blended with overcoming life-lessons and meaningful metaphors drawn and crafted from profound biblical insight.

—**Stan Gleason**, Bishop, The Life Church, Kansas City, Missouri; Assistant General Superintendent, UPCI

I've known Darin Sargent first as a student of mine for four years of college and then as a fellow minister. This book could be a history of any of us as we travel through life. It is a book for all ages, whether you are just beginning your walk with God or if you have lived many years in the church. It brings into view many things I have experienced in my sixty-six years of ministry, and you will see yourself throughout the pages. Thank you, Darin, for a book long overdue but one you perhaps better than others can express all the lions we all may face.

—**Dannie Odle**, former instructor, Christian Life College
Stockton, CA

In reading the manuscript of Darin Sargent's, *Battle the Beast: Defeating the Lions That Oppose Your Destiny*, I concluded that I have never read anything quite like it! I applaud Brother Sargent for putting his amazing thoughts, insight, and revelations into words, and I believe it will be a bestseller! I highly recommend this book to anyone who wishes to defeat the enemy's will to subvert their God-given purpose! Darin has the unique ability to keep you glued to the pages with great skill, humor, wisdom, and raw emotion, all the while implanting life-changing weapons that will result in ultimate victory.

—**Gordon Mallory**, former missionary
to the Philippine Islands

It has been said that your values are revealed through your behavior, and your behavior paves the way to your destination. Therefore, the significance of your values cannot be overstated. In *Battle the Beast*, my friend Darin Sargent addresses the mindsets that create less-than-ideal values that oppose your destiny. Join him in overcoming obstructions to becoming the person God intends you to be. You won't be disappointed.

—**Eugene Wilson**, Leadership Consultant,
President of Texas Bible College

The very word beast creates anxiety in ordinary people. To take it a step further, a beast from the unknown is the stuff of horror novels. Yet, we all encounter terrifying beasts as we walk through life. Darin Sargent has written an incredible book that you will immediately connect with! This book will help you identify hidden beasts you may be unaware of. It will also help you understand the nature of others you may be battling as you read this book. You will begin to understand, and with that knowledge, you will gain the confidence to walk carefully. Carrying the sword of the Spirit in one hand and the shield of faith in the other.

—**Michael Flowers**, Pastor, Calvary Tabernacle
San Fernando, California

BATTLE THE BEAST

Defeating the Lions That Oppose Your Destiny

DARIN SARGENT

BATTLE THE BEAST

Defeating the Lions That Oppose Your Destiny

WORD AFLAME PRESS
WELDON SPRING, MO

Word Aflame Press®
36 Research Park Court
Weldon Spring, MO 63304
pentecostalpublishing.com

© 2024 by Darin L. Sargent

All rights reserved. No portion of this publication may be reproduced, stored in an electronic system, or transmitted in any form or by any means, electronic, mechanical, photocopy, recording, or otherwise, without the prior permission of Word Aflame Press. Brief quotations may be used in literary reviews.

Unless otherwise identified, Scripture verses quoted are from the New King James Version © 1982 by Thomas Nelson, Inc. Used by permission. All rights reserved.

Scriptures marked (KJV) are from the King James Version; (ESV) from the English Standard Version © 2001 by Crossway Bibles, a publishing ministry of Good News Publishers; (NIV) from the New International Version © 1973, 1978, 1984, 2011 by Biblica, Inc.; (NLT) from the New Living Translation © 1996, 2004, 2007 by Tyndale House Foundation. Used by permission. All rights reserved.

Printed in the United States of America

Cover design by Jeremy Hart

33 32 31 30 29 28 27 26 25 24   1 2 3 4 5

Library of Congress Cataloging-in-Publication Data

Names: Sargent, Darin L., 1969- author.
Title: Battle the beast : defeating the lions that oppose your destiny / by Darin L. Sargent.
Description: Weldon Spring, MO : Word Aflame Press, [2024] | Summary: "This book provides practical ways readers can overcome many of the challenges that can stifle personal growth and fulfillment"-- Provided by publisher.
Identifiers: LCCN 2023055290 (print) | LCCN 2023055291 (ebook) | ISBN 9780757764950 (paperback) | ISBN 9780757764967 (epub)
Subjects: LCSH: Resilience (Personality trait)--Religious aspects--Christianity.
Classification: LCC BV4597.58.R47 S274 2024 (print) | LCC BV4597.58.R47 (ebook) | DDC 155.2--dc23/eng/20240206
LC record available at https://lccn.loc.gov/2023055290
LC ebook record available at https://lccn.loc.gov/2023055291

CONTENTS

Foreword xi
Preface xiii
Acknowledgments xvii
1 Introduction 1
2 Before Giants Fall 11
3 From a King's Court to a Cave 25
4 Going Beneath the Surface 37
5 The Lion of Fear 43
6 The Lion of Apathy 57
7 The Lions of Self 67
8 The Lion of Unforgiveness 83
9 The Lion of Comparison 89
10 The Lion of Mediocrity 95
11 The Lion of Entitlement 103
12 The Lion of Looking Back 111
13 The Lion of Limitations 123
14 The Lion of Temptation 131
15 The Lion of Impatience 141
16 The Lion of Deception 147
17 Stop the Mouths of Lions 153
18 A Final Word 161

FOREWORD

For me, it is quite simple. If I'm going to read a book about auto repair, I want the author to have a little grease under his fingernails. If one is going to write about gardening, then I think it necessary that his jeans be somewhat soiled from kneeling in the dirt pulling weeds. If his topic is woodworking, then he'd better know the sting of removing a splinter or two. In other words, I'm looking for life experience over theories.

By that metric (and many others), the author of *Battle the Beast* meets the threshold for me to read his work. You should too, for in it you will glean from the experience and wisdom of one whose spiritual armor demonstrates evidence of the fight. Darin Sargent is one who has experienced the hardships and "lions" of spiritual development. Born to godly parents, Darin began his days with a physical limitation that he could have readily used as an excuse to limit his Kingdom potential. Instead, it became just one of the manifold "pits" in which he slew the lions that arose from within to defeat him.

And we all have them. No matter your background, they are hiding inside you. Apathy, fear, self-doubt, and a host of other predators are ready at any moment to capitalize on a mistake you make, a hurt you experience, a disappointment

FOREWORD

you endure, or just the unfolding of life's vicissitudes. In those vulnerable moments, our inherent, fleshly tendencies pounce with the intention of stripping us of the destiny God has ordained. Thankfully, the lessons the author has learned in his battles fill the pages of the book you now hold. They are weapons available to you by which you may defeat your own personal lions.

No, you may not face the same physical limitations that the author did, but we each have our own challenges that unleash the internal "lions" of which he writes. I commend to you the observations and insights of one with grease under his spiritual nails, dirty pants' knees, and the scars of splinters. He's been there. He's battled the lions. He's conquered them. And now he exposes them for us all to see.

Read on, for your destiny awaits, lions or not. One who has faced them before will guide you on.

Scott Graham
General Secretary and Treasurer
United Pentecostal Church International

PREFACE

"Please listen to me, Darin. You'll come out of this experience stronger and better than before. It will be the very thing God uses to make you who He has called you to be."

I heard the words, yet they seemed unable to penetrate the dense fog of embarrassment, hurt, shame, and guilt that surrounded me at that moment. It felt like my world was collapsing, and I was uncertain how to respond. I was in my early twenties, just beginning to embrace God's calling on my life. I had recently navigated through one of the most challenging storms of my young life, primarily due to my own poor choices. I had allowed my inner struggles to direct my decisions.

My father was standing beside me when those words were spoken to me, and he later told me I should heed those words. He said this challenging season would eventually pass, and the lessons I learned from it would shape my future for years to come. My young age and immaturity kept me from fully comprehending the message at the time; however, looking back, I can see the wisdom in what had been spoken into my life.

This experience made me realize that personal challenges can become change agents that shape and transform our lives.

PREFACE

The result? A life divinely infused with meaning and the awareness that we are chosen to influence the lives of others.

Struggle and opposition serve as fuel for both leadership and life. Without such challenges, the force that propels personal development and the power to influence the lives of others remains dormant. The question before us is whether we will yield to internal struggles that seek to defeat us or remain steadfast in the belief that God has better designs for us and wants to help us overcome every adversary. Will we succumb to these pressures and lead a life that has little impact, or will we rise to the challenges and fulfill our potential?

No one can force you to become the person God has called you to be. If you so choose, you can observe from the sidelines and avoid the arena where your influence could make a difference. The game will go on, but the outcome will not be the same without your contribution and investment.

I grew up reading books that transported me to distant landscapes where heroes faced adversity and came out triumphant. These characters didn't start their journeys with heroism in mind; they simply walked down rugged paths, confronted immense challenges, grappled with trials and tribulations—and emerged victorious.

This book was birthed during a season of my life marked by unexpected storms and uncertainty. I'm a bit apprehensive about spilling my guts on these pages, and I'll be the first to tell you I do not have all the answers. But my deepest desire is that I can somehow convey the wisdom gleaned from personal experience, from history, and from Scripture to assist you in fully embracing your potential and becoming the person God wants you to be. If you will trust in the power of God to conquer your inner struggles, I'm confident you can overcome any obstacles and fulfill your God-ordained destiny.

PREFACE

It is essential that you overcome internal obstacles and struggles *because the issues residing within you have the potential to shape the world around you.* You must be intentional in addressing your inner world. Issues of the heart are significant. The inner realm, frequently overlooked due to its invisibility, requires attention if you want to make a meaningful impact on your family, friends, church, community, and world. Undoubtedly, beginning this process will require a significant investment, but I can guarantee you that the ultimate outcome will be an extraordinary accomplishment with the potential to reshape your life and turn you into a vessel of honor within the framework of God's divine plan.

This process begins with the power of God working within you and through you. As you confront and destroy each inner adversary, your ability to affect the world around you will expand significantly, and your purpose will become clear.

I have included study questions at the end of each chapter for two reasons.

(1) My prayer is that this book will affect you on a personal level. So grab a notebook and take time to write down your responses to the study questions. Being honest with yourself might be a challenge, but I'm confident it will lead to a transformation. Investing time in introspection is essential to identify any obstacles that are hindering your progress.

(2) Consider using these questions as a resource for a small group to foster corporate growth. There is strength in mutual accountability and the open exchange of thoughts in this type of format. Buy a copy for each member and dedicate time to exploring the chapters and responding to the questions collectively. Embrace the potential of group discussion to lead you to new and unexpected insights.

PREFACE

The Scripture conveys that the enemy may surge in like an overwhelming flood, but the Spirit of God will raise a banner against him. Therefore, embrace the presence of God in your life, even during your darkest night. Allow Him to light the way toward becoming the person He wants you to be. I am praying for you as you journey through this book, because I know He has incredible plans for your life. Extraordinary things lie ahead for you!

Keep fighting the battle!

ACKNOWLEDGMENTS

I shut my laptop, and an immediate rush of excitement overwhelmed me as if a significant weight had been lifted from my shoulders. The book was finished, or at least its initial draft was. All that remained was the daunting task of editing the manuscript and ensuring the words I had written made sense. A tall order, I know, but even though these challenges were substantial, the emotions surging through me were profound as I began to express my gratitude to God for the opportunity granted me to write this book, which I hope will bring blessings to many people.

What had initially been a fleeting idea one early summer morning, just a mere two months before I believed my book to be finished, was ready for submission to the publisher. I held my breath, praying it would be accepted and brought to life in print. I was done; it was finished, a masterpiece destined to sell a million copies! (Thanks for your purchase. We're just 999,999 copies away.)

Yet this achievement would not have been attainable without the assistance of numerous individuals, and I wish to express my gratitude before you embark on this unique journey.

ACKNOWLEDGMENTS

First, I want to say how grateful I am to my amazing wife, Duana. The Scripture still rings true: "He who finds a wife finds a good thing, and obtains favor from the Lord" (Proverbs 18:22, ESV). When God led me to you, I discovered the most exquisite gift—a divine masterpiece—that became intricately woven into the fabric of my life. You've been my unwavering companion, standing steadfastly by my side. Together, we've courageously battled the beasts that threatened to dismantle the sacred work unfolding within us. My love for you knows no bounds, and I am eternally grateful for your presence in my life.

I am also thankful for my children, Carson (married to the lovely Emily), Ashton (married to the wonderful young man, Hunter), and our youngest child, Averie. We've witnessed your growth, your resilience, and your triumphs as you have faced countless challenges. And our hearts swell with pride for each of you! Keep pressing forward, and keep fighting the good fight. You are loved beyond measure.

Mom and Dad: Without your guidance, I could never have triumphantly battled the various beasts that sought to dismantle my future. You taught me how to press forward, even when lions emerged from the pits along my journey. Your love and steadfast support have shaped me into the man I am today. I love and cherish you both and am eternally grateful for your presence by my side during many of the most intense battles of my life.

I would also like to extend my gratitude to the numerous friends who provided unwavering encouragement throughout the journey of writing this book. The list is extensive; naming everyone individually would inevitably lead to unintentional omissions. Thus, I express my sincere thanks to each one of you from the depths of my heart. I am truly blessed with many friends for whom I am eternally grateful. Your

ACKNOWLEDGMENTS

friendship, support, and encouragement have been among the greatest joys in my life.

I'd also like to extend my appreciation to Kaleb Saucer and Alena Stewart for their outstanding contributions to the marketing aspect of this book. The remarkable ideas and strategies you both effortlessly pull out of seemingly thin air are truly awe-inspiring. I am grateful for both of you and your willingness to make this dream come true. You are a gift to the body of Christ.

To Everett Gossard, my sincere thanks, my friend. Your editing skills significantly enhanced this book. Your encouragement, unique perspectives, and excellent abilities have been invaluable throughout the process. I truly appreciate your friendship. You have been a great inspiration to me, and I am so thankful for you. Get ready; we have more books to write!

In conclusion, to all of you who are reading this, thank you for acquiring this book, and I hope that you overcome every obstacle that has sought to divert you from your destiny. You are intricately crafted by a Creator deeply invested in seeing you fulfill your calling. I pray this book resonates within the depths of your heart, inspires you to stand strong amid challenges, and helps you become the overcomer I believe you are.

May God richly bless you,
Darin Sargent

1

INTRODUCTION

The true battleground lies within, where our inner struggles are most significant.

We often focus heavily on external conflicts, but the heart often poses the greatest challenges.

Life passes so swiftly that we often don't realize it until it's too late. I'm standing on the other side of the age of fifty as I write these words. My thoughts take me back to 1987 in the town of Kimberly, Idaho. The memory of that moment is etched in my mind as vividly as if it were only yesterday. I'm standing in line consumed by a mixture of anticipation and nervousness as I eagerly await the granting of my high school diploma. My heart surges with aspirations. I envision a future filled with possibilities. I gaze into the vast expanse of the unknown, standing in my belief that within its realm resides untold promises and limitless potential waiting eagerly for me.

Now let me transport you forward to 1991, another pivotal moment. I'm standing in line waiting to be called forward to receive another diploma, the tangible evidence of four enlightening yet demanding years of Bible college. In that significant moment, my dreams shimmer brightly before

INTRODUCTION

me, brimming with the potential of everything I believe will come to pass. However, as the years roll by, reality unfolds in unexpected ways, and life introduces a series of challenges that test my resolve on this journey of discovery.

Challenges have been my constant companion since my earliest childhood days. Born with what some might label a handicap or a disability, I have encountered numerous physical obstacles that many people believed I could not conquer. However, as daunting as these physical challenges were, they faded in comparison to the battles waged in the depths of my heart, within the hidden arena of darkness no one could see. These internal struggles, fears, doubts, and insecurities were the things that truly tested the strength of my spirit and my faith. Here in that unseen domain I confronted my deepest fears and fought with every ounce of courage I could muster.

Embarking on the journey to significance requires diving into the uncharted depths of challenges often unseen by others. The prophet Jeremiah boldly declared:

> The heart is deceitful above all things, and desperately wicked; who can know it? I, the LORD, search the heart, I test the mind, even to give every man according to his ways, according to the fruit of his doings. (Jeremiah 17:9–10)

In exploring our innermost selves we must battle the beast that lurks within and recognize our capacity for deceit and wickedness. Only through a deep self-understanding coupled with the divine guidance of the Lord can we conquer these challenges and grow and bear fruit. These inner victories become the crucial foundation for becoming the individual God desires us to be.

During our childhood years, life usually does not present overwhelming obstacles. Talk to children about what

INTRODUCTION

they want to be when they grow up, and you'll witness their enthusiasm as they dream of becoming astronauts, firefighters, doctors, trapeze artists (this was my future dream job, but I don't believe I thought it all the way through), or a myriad of other careers. For children, the realm of possibilities knows no bounds.

As we get older and progress through college or embark on a career path, we may hold faithfully to the expectations that our dreams will come to fruition just as we envisioned them and in the amount of time we planned. We think our impact on the lives of others will soon be recognized. Unfortunately, unforeseen struggles arise as we strive to move forward. We encounter unexpected turns in life's road—obstacles and adversaries we were never warned about in school or at home. The resistance catches us off guard, threatening to detour our advancement or bring it to a screeching halt.

However inconvenient it may be or how much we push against it, the truth remains: *It is through the struggle that life acquires profound meaning.* During the demanding journey, we discover invaluable lessons, which can be understood only when we embrace the challenges that confront us. When we adopt a posture of resilient reliance upon God, we are empowered to conquer obstacles and become the people He envisions us to be.

If you're reading these words and thinking, *I've never encountered significant challenges in my life*, consider yourself fortunate. However, for those with whom these words deeply resonate, let me offer a truth: promises are forged within the crucible of pressure. Hidden aspects within the depths of our being require attention, and unless we address them we may reach the end of life's journey filled with regret. God's ultimate desire for all of us is to achieve maturity, nurture

INTRODUCTION

our faith, and extend our impact on this world, but this will require the challenge of rigorous self-examination.

A life of impact often unfolds in the face of resistance, and this very resistance shapes the path ahead. At nineteen years of age, I penned a statement that has guided me through life:

> *You will never make an impact unless you are committed to the collision.*

In other words, the most significant *collision* we will encounter is with ourselves. I have lived by a simple principle: "I can only fix what I'm willing to face." Doubts, fears, and insecurities manifest as strong opponents seeking to deter us from reaching our full potential. But it is precisely when we confront these internal adversaries head-on that we can grow, evolve, mature, and thrive. Fighting these inner battles develops strength and resilience. Facing inner opposition helps us understand the depths of our capabilities and the power of God at work in those secret underground bunkers.

The decision to confront these challenges in your life is entirely up to you. No one else can make that choice for you. You have the option to merely exist or to truly live. If you're content with life unfolding by chance, you're simply coasting through existence. If you're satisfied with never realizing your full potential, you're opting to wander through life without truly embracing it.

My purpose behind writing this book is to encourage you to closely examine the forces that rear their ugly heads as you journey through life. Throughout this writing, I will refer to these forces as lions that lie in wait, ready to pounce at various seasons in your life. With this perspective, we adopt a proactive approach in our determination to make a significant difference in our own lives as well as the lives of others. We will acknowledge the presence of the lions that

INTRODUCTION

have remained concealed beneath the surface, awaiting the opportune moment to emerge and potentially undermine our progress.

At the time of this writing I am immersed in contemplation, reflecting on the multifaceted aspects of our family's personal journey. With two of our three children now married and my wife and I celebrating three decades of shared love and commitment, the speed at which time passes becomes increasingly evident. Have we encountered challenges? Has our journey often been marked by heartache and struggle? Have we faced insurmountable odds and questioned why things happened the way they did? The answer is a resounding *yes* on all accounts.

Undertaking this project compels me to look back over the years and ask myself, *Where has the time gone? How did we get here so quickly?* Have I faced and conquered every lion, or are there more beasts still lying in wait to destroy me or my family? It feels as if five decades of living have amounted to a mere drop in the proverbial bucket of life's experiences—and there are many more experiences ahead.

Time, as the adage goes, waits for no one. It marches to the beat of its own drum, unencumbered by considerations of personal identity, family background, or occupational pursuits. Its sole purpose is to forge ahead. Regardless of one's age or experience level, life keeps flowing like a mighty river, where, regardless of the obstacles, its irresistible current moves forward with unstoppable force. It continuously exerts pressure upon the objects in its path, determined to either dislodge the barriers or rise to such heights that it triumphantly overwhelms the obstacles.

Growing up in Idaho, my family and I had the opportunity to raft down some of the most breathtakingly beautiful rivers in the wilderness areas of the "Gem State." Together

INTRODUCTION

with my dad and brothers, we tackled the Payette River, the Salmon River, and several others that are famous for their challenging whitewater rapids. We often encountered a colossal boulder in the heart of a swiftly flowing river. At first it appeared as if the current would dislodge it, but we quickly discovered that the water would either flow over the boulder or seek an alternative path around it, pulling our raft along with it. This became a meaningful metaphor for life and the challenges we encounter.

If permitted, life has the potential to overpower and overwhelm. Its unforeseeable challenges can inflict pain and heartache, betray your trust, and provoke frustrations that resonate deep within your soul. The latter stages of many people's lives are marked with regret as they reflect on accomplishments left unattained, potential left untapped, and numerous lives left untouched by their influence. It becomes evident they could have achieved so much more if they had cultivated a mindset driven by their God-given purpose. Instead, they allowed their purpose to be crushed and buried under the pressures of life. They never experienced the transformation that God had intended.

We used to live near a zoo in Southern California called the Safari Park. Our kids loved going inside the amazing butterfly exhibit to watch as butterflies landed on their arms, heads, shoulders, legs, and shoes. Each butterfly was unique and beautiful.

Butterflies don't start out as beautiful, winged creatures that flit effortlessly through the air. Rather, they begin as caterpillars—slow and sluglike and usually overlooked unless they happen to invade your personal space. But at some point a transformation known as metamorphosis begins. This incredible demonstration of God's creative genius changes the wormy, voracious creature into a graceful, often colorful

INTRODUCTION

adult butterfly or moth. This life cycle has become a symbol of change and growth, and the beauty that can arise from it. The same can happen in each of our lives if we choose to allow God's power to work in us and conquer the forces that want to keep us defeated.

By learning to embrace life's pressures and transcend the constraints of unforeseen challenges or self-imposed limitations, we can embark on a journey to overcome the obstacles that seek to stifle our influence. Then, when we reach the end of our lives, we will hear the resounding words of affirmation: "Well done, good and faithful servant."

To effectively navigate this journey, our lives must be intentionally lived out and consistently examined so we can become the individuals God intended for us to be. If we choose not to examine ourselves—refuse to pull back the veil of our flawed perspective—we will become the conquered

Our lives must be intentionally lived out and consistently examined so we can become the individuals God intended for us to be.

instead of the conqueror. It ultimately comes down to this: the cost of nurturing and living a life of influence and impact is far less costly than facing regrets at the end of one's journey.

As you embark on this transformative journey of self-revelation, you may unearth hidden chambers where lions are lying in wait—the things you have concealed, suppressed, and buried so deep within that you may have forgotten their existence until they emerge, uninvited, during life's most inopportune moments, and inflict seemingly irreparable damage.

INTRODUCTION

I write as a fellow traveler who hasn't wholly triumphed over every lion, but I've lived long enough to recognize the vast depths beneath the surface. I understand the necessity of consistently diving deep into that realm to confront and slay the lions that lurk there. If left undefeated, those lions have the potential to hinder my progress or inflict harm upon those dear to me who may be walking a similar path.

Life is all about making a difference. If you want your life to positively impact those you are called to lead and serve, you must confront those hidden challenges that lurk beneath the surface of your being. There is no alternative route to true effectiveness. Don't fall prey to the temptations to opt for the easier path, settle for what's convenient, or yield to the pressure that genuine transformation demands. You must stand firm against the enemies that will emerge, attempting to persuade you that the effort is not worthwhile.

As we embark on this transformative journey, we will dive deep into the lives of two remarkable Old Testament individuals whose stories provide invaluable lessons: David and Benaiah. These two men, united by their experiences, offer a complete narrative of what it means to emerge triumphant out of the depths of adversity. By closely examining their lives, we will gain the insight and inspiration needed to overcome obstacles in our path.

We will also examine characters who have yet to realize the importance of tackling these dangerous creatures that dwell in pits and whose intention is to hinder and destroy lives and legacies. We will discuss prominent individuals in history and Scripture who allowed these lurking lions to remain hidden, only to emerge and wreak havoc on the destinies of those who seemed to have so much potential. These individuals illustrate the behaviors to steer clear of as

INTRODUCTION

we navigate through our transformative journey and grow into the individuals we were intended to be.

I submit that there is no loftier purpose in life than the one that beckons us to conquer ourselves. Thus, the goal of this journey is to align ourselves with God's calling and to recognize that our transformation and victory can be achieved only by courageously confronting the lions that lie hidden within. Our adversary knows that with the guidance of the Holy Spirit we are not just conquerors but more than conquerors. So the adversary fights against us, pressing on all sides to prevent us from descending into the realm of inner darkness to overcome the lions that oppose our destiny.

In our exploration and self-discovery we might come face-to-face with hideous beasts of fear or unforgiveness or mediocrity or deception. These lions, as well as many others we will discuss, symbolize both familiar and unfamiliar obstacles that await an opportune moment to hinder our potential and undermine our destiny. We will scrutinize and conquer these beasts, paving the way to fulfill our divine purpose, guide our families toward eternal fulfillment, embrace our true selves as ordained by God, and leave a lasting impact on future generations.

So join me as we begin to battle beasts.

Study Questions

1. How does the author's personal reflection on life's progression and the impact of unforeseen challenges resonate with your own experiences and perspectives on life's journey?

2. The text mentions the importance of embracing challenges and confronting the hidden battles within us. Can you share an example from your

INTRODUCTION

life where facing internal challenges led to personal growth or transformation?

3. The text refers to the metaphor of hidden lions or obstacles lurking beneath the surface. How can we proactively identify and address these internal obstacles in our own lives to fulfill our potential?

2
BEFORE GIANTS FALL

> *Then Samuel asked, "Are these all the sons you have?"*
> *"There is still the youngest," Jesse replied. "But he's out in the fields*
> *watching the sheep and goats." (I Samuel 16:11, NLT)*

Have you ever experienced a pivotal moment that altered the course of your future? A moment of such profound intensity that it etched itself within the core of your being, leaving an indelible mark upon your soul? In the blink of an eye, you realize you can never return to the person you once were. The impact of such a moment is so potent that it reshapes your perspective, aspirations, and the trajectory of your life. It causes you to recognize the hand of God guiding you to embrace a life that goes beyond mere existence.

Just such a moment can be found in the life of a young shepherd boy named David. Upon initial observation, David lacked distinguishing qualities that might have set him apart. He was initially presented as a humble shepherd boy, the lowliest occupation within his father's household. In fact, this youngest son was so inconspicuous that it never occurred to Jesse to summon him along with his older brothers to stand in the presence of Samuel.

Let's set the stage. An unprecedented day dawns upon the little town of Bethlehem with the arrival of the esteemed prophet Samuel. Apprehension grips the town elders; they're afraid this man of God has come to deliver prophetic declarations of judgment. However, as they interact with the prophet, their worries fade, for it becomes evident his purpose is not to bring alarm but to officiate at a special sacrifice to the Lord.

Samuel's secret mission is to anoint the chosen successor to the throne of Israel from among the sons of Jesse, but this little community remains oblivious to Samuel's true intention. The atmosphere crackles with intrigue and curiosity as the townspeople stand on the precipice of an extraordinary moment in their history. It is not an easy journey for Samuel; fear grips his heart at what Saul might do to him should he discover Samuel's true mission.

At first glance, selecting the next monarch to lead Israel appears deceptively simple because the options are limited. Samuel has received explicit instructions from God to choose someone from the town of Bethlehem, specifically from the family of Jesse. Samuel complies with God's instructions and extends an invitation to Jesse and his sons to partake in the sacrificial ceremony. After the sacrifice, and as Jesse's sons line up before the prophet, Samuel naturally assumes that Jesse's firstborn will be the most suitable candidate to accept the leadership over the ailing nation. Listen in on Samuel's premature assumption:

> When they arrived, Samuel took one look at Eliab and thought, "Surely this is the LORD's anointed!" (I Samuel 16:6, NLT)

Samuel stumbled into a familiar pitfall as he considered the outward appearance of Eliab and hastily assumed he must be the chosen one in God's eyes. After all, the tall firstborn son looked like a warrior. It seemed only natural that Samuel would perceive him as a potential leader, the next king of Israel.

As humans, we tend to assess a person's character based on the outward appearance. We are drawn to individuals who exude strength, excellence, courage, and power, deeming them worthy of leadership positions, as these traits often align with our perception of the qualifications for leadership.

We tend to elevate individuals based on their outward talents, abilities, confidence, or giftings while neglecting to prioritize the essence of their character and inner strength. Throughout my journey I've come to realize that the altitude of one's ascent in life can only reach the height of the distance one's character has descended into the deep. Simply put, you can only go as high as your character is deep. A focus on external talents and abilities paves the way for disappointment. When life's demands grow increasingly intense, it becomes tricky to navigate without a resilient inner foundation. As we will soon discover, things operate on a different level in God's domain.

You can only go as high as your character is deep.

As Samuel wrestled with God's instructions, God spoke to the prophet again and reminded him of an important principle:

> Don't judge by his appearance or height, for I have rejected him. The LORD doesn't see things the way you see them. People judge by outward appearance, but the LORD looks at the heart. (I Samuel 16:7, NLT)

As Samuel proceeded down the line of Jesse's sons, a disheartening realization dawned upon him—not one of them was the chosen vessel destined to become the next king of Israel. Had he heard the voice of God incorrectly? Had he taken the wrong path at the fork in the road? Samuel's frustration began to surface as he asked Jesse, "Are these all the sons you have?" Jesse's response, to paraphrase, reveals a dismissive attitude toward his youngest son: "Well, there is one more, but he's a mere shepherd boy, insignificant and unworthy of consideration."

Samuel insisted that David be brought in from the field and refused to proceed until he arrived. The moment David stepped onto the scene, God whispered to Samuel, confirming that this was indeed the chosen one, the next king of Israel. Samuel obeyed the divine instruction without hesitation and anointed David in the presence of his astonished brothers and father.

These events must have perplexed all parties involved. God's selection of the least likely candidate to ascend to the throne introduces us to yet another profound principle in the economy of the Almighty: it is the least among us who rises to greatness in God's divine plan. It is often the weak who are made strong through the power of God.

God has never required the brave or the elite, the strong or the resolute to carry out His purposes. He does not depend on a majority to accomplish His divine agenda. Instead, God derives pleasure in drawing from the melting pot of the common—the seemingly insignificant, overlooked, and undervalued individuals who at first glance may not seem like they have much to offer.

An example from history illustrates this principle. During World War II, Germany's formidable war machine had set its sights on the United Kingdom. Spearheaded by the Luftwaffe air command, Germany's relentless bombardment unleashed destruction upon the nation. But they didn't fully comprehend the indomitable spirit and resilience of Britain's Royal Air Force led by the strategic brilliance of Commander Hugh Dowding. The Royal Air Force may have appeared less prepared, equipped, or trained than the German Luftwaffe. In the eyes of Hermann Göring, the Luftwaffe commander, it seemed inconceivable that the Royal Air Force could withstand their onslaught for more than four days.

The RAF consisted of a group of young, ragtag pilots who lacked extensive training. Despite their smaller number and inferior training, their indomitable spirit prevailed. During the summer and early fall of 1940, the RAF achieved an extraordinary feat when the Battle of Britain, the first battle fought solely in air space, turned the tide of war and halted Germany's assault.

While the battle raged, Winston Churchill, in a moment of resolute determination, addressed the House of Commons with a profound proclamation: "Never in the field of human conflict was so much owed by so many to so few." Those brief words immortalized the profound gratitude of a nation and a world for the courageous few who valiantly stood against overwhelming odds to defend freedom. Flying Hurricanes and Spitfires, the young RAF pilots courageously pushed back against the onslaught of a vastly superior air command and prevented the Luftwaffe from gaining control over the skies of the English Channel. It was the first major defeat of the war for Germany and became a pivotal turning point in the war. The world witnessed the remarkable power of resilience as the young RAF pilots defied the odds and reshaped the trajectory of history.

The words of the apostle Paul to the church at Corinth resonate with wisdom: "God hath chosen the foolish things of the world to confound the wise; and God hath chosen the weak things of the world to confound the things which are mighty" (I Corinthians 1:27, KJV). God's ways often defy human logic and expectations. He delights in working through the seemingly insignificant and unremarkable, confounding the wise and mighty with His extraordinary power.

This story holds such encouragement for us today. You may believe you have nothing significant to offer the kingdom of God. Perhaps you perceive your talents and abilities as so limited that they barely register on God's heavenly radar. My dear friends, let me assure you that you possess within you far more than you can imagine. You hold something unique and valuable that God desires to utilize to profoundly impact the world around you.

Growing up, I often experienced the sharp sting of feeling excluded. I recall being overlooked, ignored, and dismissed. Even when it came to picking teams for kickball, I'd always find myself one of the last picked. I felt like shouting, "Hey, you guys, I'm not missing a foot. Come on! What's going on here?" Being born with only one hand, I often found myself gazing at what society deemed to be my "handicap," questioning why I had been destined to bear this unique condition. Little did I know in those early years that God possesses the extraordinary ability to transform our greatest disadvantages into our most powerful advantages!

Imagine yourself in David's shoes. Although he was a son, he wasn't summoned to attend the sacred sacrifice, which was actually the anointing ceremony of the next chosen king of Israel. David stood on the sidelines. Overlooked, forgotten, disregarded, left out. Little did those who were present realize that God, in His divine wisdom, was about to unveil an astonishing surprise, for on that day an insignificant shepherd boy was anointed the future monarch of Israel.

Although many years would pass before David ascended to the throne of Israel, the path he embarked upon holds significant weight in the continuation of our story. Once David was anointed as the future king of Israel, the gears of destiny began to turn. King Saul found himself being tormented by evil spirits pushing him toward madness. As the torment worsened, his courtiers searched for a musician who could soothe the king's troubled soul. One of Saul's servants caught wind of a musician with exceptional harp skills, which propelled David further along his path. God was guiding David's path even though it seemed to be a winding route.

When God has something remarkable in store for you, the path on which you embark and the time it takes to reach your destination hold little significance. He will steer you and equip you for that ultimate purpose. I'm not implying that the path or timing is insignificant; rather, I'm suggesting that sometimes we give them more importance than they deserve. It's likely that David didn't understand everything that would transpire before he eventually ascended to the throne.

Whenever the evil spirit began to torment Saul, David entered the room and, inspired by the Spirit of God, sang and played melodies that drove away the tormenting spirit, allowing Saul to regain his composure and resume his kingly duties. This continued for an extended period as David repeatedly returned home to tend to his father's sheep, only to be summoned back to Saul's court when the king's condition worsened. The duration of David's dual responsibilities is uncertain, but scholars suggest it might have lasted at least a year. David faithfully fulfilled his duties while balancing his shepherd responsibilities at home with his musical role at Saul's court.

Let us fast-forward to the Valley of Elah where an epic battle was about to be fought between the armies of Israel and the mighty Philistines. On one side stood King Saul and his once-valiant warriors, now drained of all courage. Across the valley stood the Philistine army brimming with confidence bolstered by the presence of Goliath—a colossal figure standing nine feet tall.

Amid the tense atmosphere, Goliath issued his audacious challenge, his booming voice echoing across the valley. There was no response; no Israelite soldier dared to move toward the giant. It was a humiliating moment for Israel and an embarrassment for every warrior in Saul's army, including King Saul.

It just so happened that Jesse had sent his youngest son on a simple errand to check on the welfare of his brothers who were serving in Saul's army. David carried a humble offering: a basket of roasted grain, ten loaves of bread fresh from the family oven, and ten cheeses from the family dairy. Little did he know he was about to be thrust into the midst of an intense drama. He arrived just as the army was going out to face the Philistines. He found his brothers, and as he was greeting them, a giant emerged from the Philistine ranks and began taunting the armies of Israel. Observing the tension-filled standoff, David inquired, "What is the reward that awaits the one who triumphs over this uncircumcised man from Gath?"

Some may find this situation amusing in view of the fact David was an overconfident youngster inexperienced in battle. The military men sneered as David's big brother pulled him aside to rebuke him:

> Now Eliab his eldest brother heard when he spoke to the men. And Eliab's anger was kindled against David, and he said, "Why have you come down? And with whom have you left those few sheep in

the wilderness? I know your presumption and the evil of your heart, for you have come down to see the battle." (I Samuel 17:28, ESV)

David was undeterred, declaring, "What have I done now? Is there not a cause?"

David understood this was no ordinary challenge. He recognized it as an attack against the people of God, and he knew that someone needed to rise up and defend the Lord's honor. It was a cause worth fighting for.

Perhaps you feel like you've been in David's shoes. You feel a divine calling to do something great, yet you face the scorn and disapproval of others. You sense the tangible disdain of enemies and peers who disagree with the path God has set before you. Stay steadfast and unwavering in your faith, for the God who initiated this good work in you will bring it to completion. Trust in His ways. Even if you cannot see His hand at work, trust in His heart. Believe that God will accomplish something remarkable through you. Don't let anyone convince you otherwise. Embrace the purpose He has ignited within your heart, and use that spark to set fire to your faith and dedication. You will witness the manifestation of God's greatness in and through your life.

Given the circumstances of my birth, it would have been easy for me to settle for a life of mediocrity, to blend in with the status quo. It would have been expected for me to remain on the sidelines, never daring to step onto the field of action. People would have understood if I had filled my life with excuses, but I refused to do so because God had instilled within me a resounding conviction that proclaimed, "There is a cause!"

Early on, I realized God had a purpose for my life intricately interwoven with how I was born. However, uncovering that purpose took a lot of work; it didn't happen in a single moment of revelation. I often questioned the circumstances of my birth, wondering how everything fit into God's plan. Amid the doubts and uncertainties I began to grasp that God was molding me into the person I was destined to be through resistance and struggles that allowed me to emerge stronger and more aware of my identity and purpose. The journey to self-discovery and understanding was not without challenges, but I learned to embrace them as opportunities for growth and development. Each obstacle I encountered was a chance to grow in faith and rely on God's guidance. As I walked this path, I discovered that God's plan for me was not merely about achieving success; it was about becoming the person He intended me to be. I learned to trust in His shaping process and to find strength in His unfailing love.

Being a vessel fit for God's use is important and necessary, but it is temporary. On the other hand, being transformed by God holds eternal significance. Through this transformation, God discerns how He can entrust and use us for His glory. Some people desire to be used by God mainly because it thrusts them into the limelight, boosts their followers on social media platforms like Instagram, TikTok, or whatever the current platform may be, and inflates their sense of importance beyond its true measure. Let me put this simply: God is more interested in changing us than He is in using us. If we can keep this in mind, the impact we create as we undergo the transformation process will be more

God is more interested in changing us than He is in using us.

significant, because God can use us without fearing our pride will cause complications and destroy our influence.

Looking back, I'm grateful for the resistance and struggles I faced because they molded me into the person I am today. They shaped my character, deepened my faith, and opened my eyes to the beauty of God's purpose for my life. Although the journey was challenging, I now walk forward confidently, knowing that God's hand has guided me every step of the way. And I am determined to do something that will last beyond my lifetime and continue to make a meaningful impact in the lives of others.

I know of countless people who have reached pivotal seasons in their lives only to be overtaken by the unresolved darkness that lurks within. It is disheartening to see how a refusal to confront and address deep-rooted issues ultimately leads to a downfall, impacting not only individuals but also families. That's why it's so important for us to conquer these inner beasts so we can walk in true effectiveness and fulfillment.

David's persistence paid off. He finally obtained an audience with King Saul and boldly shared his experiences and insights. David did not yield to the pressure of conforming to the king's expectations. Instead, he confidently recounted his victories over a lion and a bear, conveying to Saul that despite his lack of military prowess, he was equipped to face this giant. It was as if David was assuring Saul, "I have faced some frightening opponents before, and God has empowered me to overcome them. I am prepared for this battle, and I don't need your armor."

Do not overlook the importance of small beginnings. Though facing a lion and a bear may appear insignificant compared to the daunting task of confronting a towering warrior like Goliath, those encounters were essential in preparing David for the ultimate triumph. The victory over the lion and the bear served as tangible evidence of God's faithfulness and power, instilling in David the assurance that God would grant him triumph over the uncircumcised Philistine as well. These two victories before the giant fell played a pivotal role in shaping David's confidence in God.

In the face of Saul's insistence on equipping David with unfamiliar armor, the shepherd boy's unwavering trust in God shone through. It took immense faith to reject the king's request and refuse to wear the armor of a seasoned warrior. David understood he couldn't fight his battle by imitating someone else's approach.

One of the greatest obstacles we encounter in life is the temptation to emulate others and fight our battles using someone else's methods. God created each of us as unique individuals with our own experiences and lessons learned. These experiences are the ingredients necessary to overcome challenges and achieve victory.

The battles we face are not trivial matters, but they hold the key to unlocking our future destiny. The obstacles that stand in our way often have deep roots. And these roots hinder our growth and prevent us from fully embracing who God has called us to be.

In the face of overwhelming odds, David's unwavering faith and unyielding trust in God propelled him forward. He recognized that external circumstances, no matter how intimidating, could never outweigh the power of God's purpose in his life. This is why David could face such a menacing foe and see the victory come to pass for God's chosen people.

David emerged victorious over Goliath armed with a simple sling and a single stone. What had instilled fear and trepidation in the hearts of many now lay defeated on the ground, leaving the Philistines astounded and bewildered by the sight. David ran and stood over the fallen giant. He unsheathed the heavy sword, raised it high, and cut off the head of his defeated foe. Instead of keeping the head as a trophy, David carried it, not to his hometown of Bethlehem, but to Jerusalem.

In carrying the head of Goliath to Jerusalem, David may have symbolized the future victory that would be his when he ascended to the throne. It seemed he was envisioning Jerusalem as the jewel in God's kingdom, a city destined to be captured from the Jebusites and established as a significant stronghold. David's act of faith established a pattern that played out repeatedly in his life. He was committed to trusting God for his future, family, and reason for being alive. This one action served as a powerful act of faith in God's promises and his confident anticipation of the future greatness of Israel as a nation.

In our journey through life, we may encounter challenges and obstacles that seem insurmountable. Factors such as age, talent, ability, or even our maturity level may limit our ability to conquer those challenges. Can we, like David, confront the obstacles that stand in our way and symbolically place the head of our past victories at the gate of our future? It would be a potent reminder to our adversaries that we will return even stronger and with greater determination.

The battles you confront now will pave the way for future victories. Resolve to confront and overcome what appear to be insignificant battles in your life today, thus avoiding a full-fledged war on the battlefield tomorrow. Though we may not have it all figured out at this moment, we confidently proclaim that we will fulfill the destiny God has prepared for us. Key acts of faith can set the trajectory for the rest of your life and serve as stepping stones toward fulfilling your divine destiny.

As you work through the pages of this book, I pray you will recognize the necessity of confronting the hidden, uncomfortable aspects of your life that reside in the depths, for it is in facing these hidden adversaries that true transformation and breakthroughs can occur. May you be empowered to rise above surface-level distractions and venture into the depths where your greatest victories await.

Study Questions

1. Can you recall a moment in your life when an unexpected event or encounter profoundly impacted your future? How did it shape your perspective and aspirations?

2. The author emphasizes the importance of inner character and the tendency to judge people by their outward appearance. Can you share a personal experience when you or someone you know learned the significance of inner strength and character in facing life's challenges?

3. In your own journey, how can you apply the principle highlighted in the text that "the Lord looks at the heart"? What steps can you take to prioritize inner character and strength over external qualities or talents in your life and decision-making?

3

FROM A KING'S COURT TO A CAVE

And everyone who was in distress, everyone who was in debt, and everyone who was discontented gathered to him. So he became captain over them. (I Samuel 22:2)

It's interesting to observe how success attracts attention and curiosity. King Saul's interest in David was piqued as soon as Goliath fell. The king eagerly sought to know the background of this young man. He asked Abner, his commander-in-chief, "To what family does this young man belong? Where is he from? Who is his father?"

His curiosity wasn't appeased until Abner appeared with David, still clutching the severed, bloody head of Goliath. King Saul asked about David's lineage. Standing tall, David confidently responded, "I am the son of Jesse from Bethlehem." This pivotal meeting marked the beginning of a new chapter in David's life, intertwining his humble origins with his remarkable future.

From this moment onward, David was brought into the court of King Saul, no longer returning to his father's house to tend the sheep. David embarked on a journey of success, accomplishing every mission entrusted to him by Saul. His victories in battle soon caught Saul's attention, and the king appointed him as a leader in his army. This elevation in status was well received among the people and among Saul's servants. The stage was set for David's ascent to prominence and the unfolding of his royal destiny in the Kingdom of Israel.

The streets echoed with songs of praise for David's military triumphs. The women celebrated in song, declaring Saul had conquered thousands, but David had triumphed over tens of thousands. Jealousy began growing like a cancer in the heart of King Saul. Instead of rejoicing over David's successes, Saul suffered fits of insecurity and anger. This shift transformed what should have been a season of greatness for David into a dark and frightening nightmare.

Saul's jealousy continued to intensify until his anger reached a boiling point. One day while David was playing the harp in King Saul's court, Saul hurled a javelin at him, attempting to pin him against the wall and end his life. Remarkably, David managed to evade the deadly projectile. (See I Samuel 18:11; 19:10.)

The people of Judah and Israel loved David, held him in high esteem, and recognized his numerous victories in battle. Saul's envy continued to grow in proportion to David's growing reputation, so he devised a cunning plan to eliminate David. He offered David his oldest daughter in marriage, hoping to entice him into a dangerous battle against the Philistines. Aware of his humble origins, David hesitated. He felt unworthy of the privilege of marrying into the royal family. In a cruel twist, Saul broke his promise to David by giving his oldest daughter to another man.

When Saul learned of his daughter Michal's love for David, he recognized an opportunity to manipulate the situation to even greater advantage. He would use Michal's affection for David to entrap him. Saul informed David of his intention to give Michal to him in marriage, expecting David to reject the offer. To Saul's delight, David did decline, citing his inability to meet the dowry requirement. Saul then proposed an extravagant payment for the bride price—the foreskins of one hundred Philistines killed in battle. The king believed this demand would undoubtedly lead to David's death, putting an end to the perceived threat.

Saul yet again underestimated God's favor upon David. Instead of being eliminated, David triumphed over the Philistines, solidifying his status as a mighty warrior and a force to be reckoned with in the eyes of the king. Moreover, David surpassed the king's demand by returning with two hundred Philistine foreskins as proof of his victory. Once again, the nation was singing David's praise. Saul's evil mood sank to a new low; he actively began plotting David's assassination.

Unbeknownst to Saul, his own son Jonathan had developed a deep friendship with David. Loyal and righteous Jonathan could not bear to see his friend harmed. He courageously confronted his father, reminding him of David's numerous victories, including the defeat of Goliath. Jonathan appealed to Saul's sense of reason, emphasizing that David had done nothing to harm him. Instead, he had proven himself to be a faithful, valiant servant. Jonathan's words were a powerful testimony of David's character and his loyalty to Saul. In this critical moment, the bond of friendship between the king's son and the former shepherd boy became a source of hope and protection for David, as Jonathan risked his own safety to stand up for his friend.

As you navigate life's battles, surround yourself with close friendships that will empower and support you through whatever challenges you encounter. While they may not be able to fight your battles for you, true friends can stand by your side and offer comfort and strength during times of loneliness, weariness, or fear caused by the enemy seeking to hinder your destiny. These bonds of friendship provide encouragement, reminding you that you are not alone in the journey. Together you can face the trials and triumphs, knowing that genuine friendships are gifts that sustain and uplift you throughout life's journey. Cherish those connections and let them be a source of strength, guidance, and joy as you pursue what lies ahead.

David's return to favor was short-lived as Saul's anger toward him reignited. Despite making a promise to his son Jonathan not to harm David, Saul's spear remained ever close at hand. It serves as a chilling reminder of the danger that lurks in the presence of those who harbor ill intentions.

We must exercise caution and discernment in our interactions with individuals who metaphorically may carry a spear in their hand. These are the people who seek to sabotage our dreams, quench our passion, and hinder the fulfillment of God's plan for our lives. They may be fueled by jealousy and envy toward those who excel, much like Saul's attitude toward David.

Saul's actions reveal the destructive nature of leadership driven by insecurity and envy. Instead of embracing and nurturing the potential of those around him, Saul succumbed to the darkness within his heart. His downfall began when he started waging public attacks on the one he perceived as a personal threat.

The path ahead for David took a dramatic turn; he found himself a fugitive in his own land, forced into hiding due to King Saul's relentless pursuit. David's name appeared on Israel's Most Wanted list, and Saul searched for him relentlessly. In the midst of the turmoil, a divine intervention unfolded, as the Scriptures attest, "And Saul sought him every day, *but God did not give him into his hand*" (I Samuel 23:14, ESV, emphasis added).

Despite Saul's relentless efforts, the protective hand of God remained upon David and prevented his capture. Even in the face of danger and uncertainty, David found peace in the knowledge that his destiny was in the hands of the One who holds all things together.

It has always amazed me that the enemy cannot destroy you or even detour you when God has a plan for your life. The enemy may try to divert or destroy you, but if you stay steadfast and secure in God's will, He will open up a pathway that leads to your purpose. The road will more than likely be lined with obstacles and hardship; however, rest assured "that God, who began the good work within you, will continue his work until it is finally finished on the day when Christ Jesus returns" (Philippians 1:6, NLT). You will come out on the other side victorious.

The Insecurity of Saul

A closer examination of the life of Saul uncovers some valuable lessons. As the story begins, we are introduced to a deep fissure in the character and heart of Saul; this young man's main concern was how he appeared in front of the people of God. It soon became evident that Saul sought approval and validation from others rather than relying on God's guidance. His kingship started with promise and potential, but he allowed insecurity, pride, and jealousy to overtake him, a failure that eventually ripped the reign out of his hands and destroyed his legacy. Saul's failure to address issues simmering beneath the surface, coupled with his desperate quest for the approval of others, led him astray.

As I reflect on the stark contrast between the king and the youthful shepherd, one question emerges: How did David succeed where Saul had failed? David's triumph over internal battles was rooted in his unwavering faith in God. A deep connection with God marked David's life, nurtured through his time as a shepherd boy. While Saul sought the approval of others and succumbed to the pressures of the world, David placed his trust in the Almighty and sought His guidance for every step. He learned to depend on the Lord's strength and developed a profound understanding of God's power and sovereignty. He sought to please his Creator and aligned himself with God's will. This unyielding devotion allowed him to rise above the daunting challenges he faced.

As Saul spiraled into darkness, David's faith illuminated his path and enabled him to overcome his own doubts and insecurities. He refused to let the opinions of others dictate his identity or purpose, choosing instead to embrace the person God had created him to be. While Saul's story serves as a cautionary tale of the perils of seeking human approval, David's life radiates with the power of divine guidance and unwavering trust. His triumph over doubt and fear stands as a testament to the remarkable force of faith—the kind of faith that turns trials into stepping stones that lead to triumph.

The Hiding Years

David's life became a whirlwind of escape and evasion. Over a period that may have lasted up to seven years, David wandered from one corner of the nation to another, seeking protection from Saul's wrath. Yet even amid the turmoil, God worked in remarkable ways through David, shaping him into a leader of great significance.

As the nation deteriorated under Saul's rule and his diabolical pursuit of David, a pattern began to unfold. Men who were discontented, in debt, and distressed—misfits of society—began seeking solace and purpose. Their paths led them to the cave of a warrior who had experienced the bitter sting of rejection by the man who was not only his king, but also his father-in-law. These dejected men, kicked to the curb by life, found refuge in the company of a man whom God was shaping into a future king. Together they formed an unlikely band of brothers, bound by destiny and united in their journey toward an extraordinary future.

David took these disdained, derelict men and accomplished what no one else could have achieved: he turned them into "the mighty men of David," a group of once-mediocre misfits who developed into warriors and leaders of exceptional ability.

These mighty men played a pivotal role in shaping the destiny of their nation. In the face of insurmountable odds, these extraordinary individuals secured victory for the people of God and left an indelible mark on their nation's history. Their unwavering loyalty to David and their commitment to the purpose set before them made them invaluable assets in the unfolding story of Israel.

David possessed a unique ability to ignite a fire within the hearts of these men, inspiring them to greatness. Among this extraordinary group of men stands a figure of exceptional significance: Benaiah. But before we consider Benaiah, let us first visit the refuge of Adullam, which housed not only David's mighty men, but also his family. Within the walls of this vast cavern, something transformative occurred, compelling those who sought shelter there to witness David's unyielding dedication to serve his generation. David must have recounted the tales of his triumphs, how he defeated lions and bears, how he bravely faced Goliath with nothing more than a sling and a stone, and how he placed Goliath's head at the gate of Jerusalem as a testament to God's power—both present and future. The passion and courage in David's voice must have kindled an unshakable sense of purpose in the hearts of those who surrounded him in the cave.

FROM A KING'S COURT TO A CAVE

We've all found ourselves in dark caves during uncertain times. Some of these caves were the result of our choices, while others were imposed upon us by external circumstances. Undoubtedly, the Adullam Cave Hotel was far from ideal for David; it wasn't a five-star resort with room service amenities or scented towels. It was a place of discomfort and necessity. Though challenging, these moments serve a purpose in our journey; they prepare us for a greater calling.

I'd like to take a moment to dispel some misconceptions about caves. We should never see them as a place of punishment or isolation but rather as a crucible where destiny molds us into the person God has called us to be. Instead of trying to escape from the cave, we should embrace it as a place of growth and transformation. Within its depths we will find the strength and guidance needed for the challenging days ahead. Our attitude is crucial during life's darkest moments because it determines what is cultivated in our lives and in the lives of those we are attempting to lead and impact.

None of us enjoy the cave seasons we encounter in life. But frequently, our most challenging wilderness and cave seasons, despite their painful appearance, become the precious gems we mine later in life. Embracing the cave, we can all develop into the individuals God has destined us to become.

If you find yourself in a cave, questioning why you're suffering through current circumstances, I encourage you to remain steadfast and embrace every lesson God presents to you during this season. Take careful note of the insights gained from each trial. Persevere like a valiant soldier, and I assure you that God will reward your faithfulness. Trust that these experiences are shaping you for a purpose beyond what you can see, and hold on to the hope that God is preparing you for something remarkable.

FROM A KING'S COURT TO A CAVE

During his stay in Adullam, David assumed the leadership of a formidable band of four hundred men. Together, they underwent growth and transformation, evolving into the mighty warriors who supported David. Yet, despite their increasing strength and preparation for the future, every move they made was discovered and reported back to Saul. The king never wavered in his pursuit. The pressure remained relentless on David and his men, but the pressure didn't stop their ranks from swelling to over six hundred.

Jonathan sought out David in the wilderness to deliver a warning. He told David that Saul was determined to end David's life. Let's eavesdrop on the heartfelt conversation between these two covenant friends in the middle of the wilderness:

> One day near Horesh, David received the news that Saul was on the way to Ziph to search for him and kill him. Jonathan went to find David and encouraged him to stay strong in his faith in God. "Don't be afraid," Jonathan reassured him. "My father will never find you! You are going to be the king of Israel, and I will be next to you, as my father, Saul, is well aware." So the two of them renewed their solemn pact before the LORD. Then Jonathan returned home, while David stayed at Horesh. (I Samuel 23:15–18, NLT)

Following this encounter with Jonathan, a critical moment unfolded as David and his men took refuge in the stronghold of En-Gedi. As fate would have it, Saul took a break from his pursuit of David and entered a cave to relieve himself. He was unaware that David and his men were hiding in the recesses of that very cave. David's men viewed this as a divine opportunity to end their suffering by killing Saul. They urged David to take advantage of the situation, claiming that God had delivered their enemy into their hands. However, David rejected the temptation to harm Saul, responding instead with unwavering integrity and respect for God's anointed king.

What had appeared to be an opportunity for vengeance became a test and a teachable moment for David's mighty men. David's decision not to harm Saul exemplified the true character of the future king who upheld God's anointing above personal ambitions. This powerful lesson reinforced the values and principles that guided these mighty men toward becoming influential leaders.

David stealthily approached Saul in the cave and cut a piece out of the hem of the king's robe. As Saul departed the cave, David called out to him, proclaiming his loyalty and informing the king of the opportunity he had passed up to take Saul's life. In a rare moment of vulnerability and transparency, Saul acknowledged God's hand was upon David and that he would become Israel's next king.

Despite Saul's tearful acknowledgment that David would be the next king, and his emotional plea asking David not to destroy his descendants, Saul continued his relentless pursuit of David. When news arrived that David was hiding out in the hills of Hachilah, Saul assembled a force of three thousand men and set out to capture him.

One night David and Abishai crept into Saul's camp where the king lay sleeping, surrounded by Abner and all his men. Abishai urged David to take Saul's life, but David once again refused, saying, "The LORD forbid that I should stretch out my hand against the LORD's anointed. But please, take now the spear and the jug of water that are by his head, and let us go" (I Samuel 26:11).

Even in the face of Saul's persistent aggression, David maintained his unwavering respect for God's anointed, choosing instead to uphold his principles and trust in divine providence rather than taking matters into his own hands. The outcome showcased the contrast between David's steadfastness and Saul's stubbornness as the two men pursued their destinies.

This narrative serves as a reminder of the importance of addressing the lions that oppose our destiny during critical moments in life. It is crucial to identify these adversaries and learn how to defeat and overcome their destructive influence. By understanding and facing these challenges head-on, we can navigate our path toward fulfilling our destiny with greater strength and purpose.

Study Questions

1. What was your response to David's choice of taking Goliath's head to Jerusalem?

2. The loyalty and friendship between Jonathan and David is one that we should pattern in our own lives. Do you have a friend like this in your life? Reach out to this friend with thanks for the impact he or she has had on your life.

3. What did you think of the statement that Saul's spear was never far from his hand? Have you ever experienced this type of relationship in your life? Talk about it with a friend or write it down to pray over in the days ahead.

4

GOING BENEATH THE SURFACE

There was also Benaiah son of Jehoiada, a valiant warrior from Kabzeel. He did many heroic deeds, which included killing two champions of Moab. Another time, on a snowy day, he chased a lion down into a pit and killed it. (II Samuel 23:20, NLT)

David's mighty men etched their names in the annals of legend and lore. Take, for example, Shammah, who stood his ground in the middle of a bean patch, singlehandedly (no pun intended) defeating the enemy attempting to seize his field. His courage turned the tide of battle and safeguarded what belonged to him and his people.

Then there was Eleazar, who stood shoulder to shoulder with David, defeating the Philistines when the rest of Israel's army retreated. He fought so long that by the end of the battle his hand clung to his sword, becoming one with it.

These were no ordinary men! They were strong and dependable—the kind of men you want by your side when facing the fiercest challenges. In the words of one of my favorite authors, Louis L'Amour, these were men to ride the river with. They may have come to David broken and dysfunctional, but they stood fiercely loyal to David, playing a vital role in establishing the kingdom God had destined him to lead.

GOING BENEATH THE SURFACE

Indeed, John Donne's saying that "no man is an island, entire of itself" holds great truth. Our connections and relationships play a significant role in shaping our lives. Many may believe they can navigate life alone and make a difference in their world without support, but the reality is that we all need others. We need mentors and guides to show us the way and lead us to reach our full potential through effective leadership. In other words, we all need a hand.

At the same time, we must be willing to extend a helping hand to those coming after us, empowering them to become all they were created to be. David's life exemplifies the essence of effective leadership, which instills a passion for serving others and makes a lasting impact on those around us.

It took me some time to realize that, despite the circumstances of my birth, I am called to make a difference in the world. Lest anyone should think I'm boasting, let me share the words of David, who recognized that we were fearfully and wonderfully made and that God knew every aspect of our being even before we were conceived. This profound understanding carries through to the New Testament, where Paul's letter to the Ephesian church continues to affirm the uniqueness and purpose that each of us holds. He wrote:

> For we are his workmanship, created in Christ Jesus for good works, which God prepared beforehand, that we should walk in them. (Ephesians 2:10, ESV)

I made up my mind a long time ago to align myself with God's ultimate plan for my life. Mediocrity and the status quo will never dominate my journey. I reject the idea of settling for an ordinary or unremarkable existence. I am a beloved child of the Almighty, fully dedicated to realizing the blessings and potential He has destined for me. With steadfast faith, I welcome the path ahead, understanding that God's purpose for my life is nothing short of remarkable.

The same can be said about you! Never forget your immense value to God and His kingdom. You are not a mere speck of dust on this spinning planet; you are precious and have a meaningful purpose to fulfill. Never underestimate the divine plans God has in store for you, the remarkable things He intends to accomplish through you, and the transformative changes He seeks to bring about within you. You are deeply loved. No matter the challenges you face, the conditions of your birth, or the pain of your past, remember that the One who started a good work in you will bring it to completion. Keep trusting and believing in God's divine plan for your life.

I firmly believe that David lived his life exactly this way. It's no wonder people were drawn to him. His captivating influence extended through the works these mighty men achieved and their profound impact on the world around them. We are called to follow David's example and make a deliberate choice to influence the lives of others.

In the historical records of David's mighty men, mentioned in both II Samuel 23 and I Chronicles 11, Benaiah's name stands out among them. Notably, his defeat of two formidable Moabite warriors, described as lionlike men, left an indelible mark in Israel's history and contributed to David's decision to elevate him to a position of honor and authority. Though the specifics of this encounter may be subject to interpretation, it is evident that these adversaries were exceptionally skilled fighters, and Benaiah's victory over them showcased his bravery and skill in battle.

But that's not all. Benaiah faced a giant Egyptian warrior armed with a massive spear. In an awe-inspiring display of strength and creativity, Benaiah managed to disarm his opponent, using only an ordinary staff. He turned the tide of the battle and used the giant's own weapon against him, ultimately slaying him with it. Benaiah was definitely someone to avoid tangling with. While Benaiah's previous feats were undeniably impressive and showcased the caliber of men David cultivated during his time of exile, what he did next holds particular significance for our narrative.

Benaiah was tending to daily duties when he unexpectedly encountered a lion. It was snowing that day, and the inclement weather made it far from an ideal moment to confront a lion. We are not sure how this all played out. Perhaps the pit on Benaiah's property was a cistern covered over by branches; maybe the pit had been previously dug to trap an animal; maybe it was just a hole in the ground. In any case, Benaiah had no intention of letting that lion roam the countryside, preying on livestock or even children. The lion took a wrong step and fell into the pit.

If it had been me, I probably would have rejoiced, done a praise dance, and quickly moved on, cherishing the safety of my one intact hand! (I am already short-handed; I don't need another appendage missing.) But Benaiah's response was quite different. Despite the challenging conditions and the danger of facing a lion in a slippery pit on a cold winter's day, Benaiah lowered himself into that pit. He understood a profound lesson we must all grasp: if I don't address this issue *while it remains hidden beneath the surface*, it could resurface unexpectedly in the future, posing a risk to myself, someone walking this same path, or someone I deeply care about.

Benaiah had every excuse to dismiss this moment with destiny: the ground was slippery, the cold was biting, and snowfall was relentless. These weather conditions are typically the perfect excuse for cozying up by a warm fire with a cup of hot cocoa and a good book—not to tackle a lion! This narrative tells us there will never be a perfect season to confront our hidden beasts that lurk beneath the surface. But if we avoid facing them while they are still hidden, they have the potential to cause significant damage later. Sometimes you must seize the opportunity and face them head-on!

Benaiah's actions on that decisive day impart a vital lesson—we cannot underestimate issues because they aren't immediately apparent. The enemy employs cunning tactics to deceive us regarding these issues. I believe there are at least two reasons to support this deception:

1. The enemy tries to persuade us that since no one else is aware of these prevailing problems, there is no urgency to address them. It does no harm to keep them concealed; we can just let sleeping lions lie.

2. The enemy attempts to convince us that we can safely postpone dealing with these matters. He downplays the potential danger they pose to us as they lie dormant beneath the surface.

It is vital we confront the threats lurking beneath the surface before they escalate into widespread devastation. Time is not on our side when dealing with issues that lie in wait, ready to strike and take us down.

It can be challenging to confront issues such as pride, lust, envy, jealousy, anger, and other potential threats. However, ignoring these challenges now will result in future generations being burdened with battles they were not meant to fight. We must overcome these challenges and eliminate them so future generations can confidently walk their path to destiny without being consumed by the same struggles.

GOING BENEATH THE SURFACE

Benaiah's courageous act of going down into the pit with the lion on that cold, snowy day is an example we should follow. Today's confrontation with the lions that oppose us will determine our victories tomorrow.

In the following chapters we will examine many of these hidden adversaries. We will uncover the obstacles holding us back and discover how to overcome them. It's time to equip ourselves, grab our spears, and prepare for battle, for we know that the One within us is greater than anything that can come against us!

Are you ready?

Let's go!

Study Questions

1. How does the story of Benaiah's confrontation with the lion on a snowy day serve as a powerful metaphor for addressing hidden challenges in our lives?

2. Why is it emphasized that there is never a perfect season to confront the threats lurking beneath the surface? How does the narrative encourage us to seize the opportunity to face these challenges, even when conditions are less than ideal?

3. In what ways can addressing the hidden challenges within us have a positive impact on future generations? How does Benaiah's example underscore the importance of confronting these issues promptly and diligently?

5

THE LION OF FEAR

For God has not given us a spirit of fear,
but of power and of love and of a sound mind. (II Timothy 1:7)

The spirit of fear lies beneath the surface, demanding your attention. At every turn and in every phase of life, this lurking lion has no qualms about rising up and confronting you with a roar. This lion doesn't care who you are or how much you want to pursue your dreams. It will show no mercy. It will raise its ugly head and try to intimidate you, silence you, and prevent you from creating a life of significance. Its sole purpose is to thwart your success and hinder you from taking the first step forward.

Many people live with fear as a constant companion, and they often feel powerless to loosen its grip. By discussing fear and exploring ways to conquer it, we can equip ourselves with the tools and knowledge needed to live a life free from the chains of fear. As we move forward, we can discover the strength to face our fears head-on and lead a life filled with courage and purpose.

As I started writing this book, I faced the challenge of deciding which lion to address first. After thorough consideration, I created a list of many lurking lions, and this one stood out to me as the hardest.

THE LION OF FEAR

Fear often serves as the root of other issues. Fear breeds doubt, insecurity, and anxiety. When fear takes hold, it has the power to paralyze us, hinder our progress, and keep us from taking necessary steps toward success. Thus, confronting and conquering fear is paramount to our purpose.

I discovered early on I couldn't allow my limb difference to determine my outlook on life. I had to face fear, as intimidating as it was at times. I recognized that fear had the potential to hold me captive in a cycle of inaction and complacency, preventing me from embracing the abundant life. So I dealt with it. By confronting fear head-on, I discovered a strength and resilience that propelled me to live a purposeful and fulfilling life. I decided I would never allow fear to dominate my future.

In recent years, I have heard people say, "It is what it is" as a response to a challenging situation or unexpected circumstance. I disagree with this philosophy. It never has to be just "what it is"! We have the power to transform any situation through our authority in Christ, so why should we settle for the status quo? Why should we succumb to fear and refrain from pressing forward? Why should we allow ourselves to roll over like a possum and play dead when we are called to do so much more with our lives?

Embracing the truth of our identity in Christ enables us to overcome adversity and defy the limitations that surround us. We can refuse to be confined by our present condition because we possess the authority and ability to effect positive change in our circumstances. In Christ, we find the courage to advance, to pursue our God-given destiny, and to overcome every obstacle in our path. Instead of passively accepting our circumstances, let us rise with faith and determination, knowing that with Christ we can shape our future and walk boldly into the life He has prepared for us.

THE LION OF FEAR

In his counsel to Timothy, his young protégé in the gospel, Paul emphasized, "For God hath not given us the spirit of fear; but of power, and of love, and of a sound mind" (II Timothy 1:7, KJV).

The understanding that fear does not originate from God calls for an examination of its true source. From Paul's advice to Timothy, we discover that fear is a spiritual matter, requiring a spiritual approach for resolution. Merely recognizing that fear is harmful is insufficient; we must take up spiritual weapons such as prayer, fasting, a devoted study of the Word of God, and a life surrendered to Christ to overcome its grip on us.

Fear's grip is unlike any other challenge we encounter in life. Its destructive force knows no bounds. It wreaks havoc on individuals, families, marriages, and even ministries. Its insidious presence can undermine our faith, cripple our progress, and hinder us from embracing the fullness of life. If left unchecked, fear can devastate every aspect of our existence, robbing us of joy, peace, and fulfillment.

Overcoming fear is crucial to living boldly and victoriously while embracing God's abundant life. It is time to face this formidable lion, break free from its grasp through faith, and step boldly into the boundless possibilities that await us. By conquering the lion of fear, we release ourselves from the chains that hold us back and set ourselves on the path to fulfilling our true destiny.

The first significant observation I've made concerning fear is its *paralyzing effect* on those it controls. Like a lion, fear holds its victims in the jaws of immobility, preventing them from taking any steps toward fulfilling their potential. I have witnessed individuals with immense talent and ability being frozen in place by the lion of fear, never daring to move forward in pursuit of their dreams. As children of God, we are designed to embrace a life of progress, growth, and purposeful action. In a world where fear seeks to immobilize, we must step boldly into the unknown, trusting in the One who goes before us and empowers us to overcome any hindrance that seeks to hold us back.

Second, it is crucial to recognize that fear has a *sterilizing effect* on those it ensnares—it hinders people from bearing fruit in their lives. If you are not vigilant, fear can prevent you from making the impact you were destined to have on the world around you. God has designed and created us to make a positive impact and bear fruit in our lives.

I grew up in the farming country of Southern Idaho, surrounded by fields in an area known as the Magic Valley. Each year the farmers anticipated a bountiful harvest of crops such as corn, potatoes, beans, or alfalfa. Imagine if one of those farmers worked himself into a dither, wondering if he should sow any seed. "What if it's a bad year for bugs? What if there's no rain? What if the soil has lost its fertility?"

Many individuals frequently experience anxiety over "what ifs" in their daily lives.

For instance, they may ask themselves, "What if God's Word isn't true? What if I commit my life to God, but He doesn't take care of me? What if I give sacrificially but I don't receive any blessings in return? What if I dedicate my life to serving God but nothing happens?"

Thankfully, most farmers choose to take a positive course of action. They confidently buy the seed, prepare the soil, and sow the seed. Their weapon against fear is their faith. They trust in the principle of sowing and reaping that has helped them succeed in the past, and they have faith that the principle will hold true this time as well. They are confident the rain will come, the seed will germinate, and the soil will furnish the vital nutrients. They plan, plow, and plant the

THE LION OF FEAR

crop with faith to guide them. But the farmer who yields to fear and chooses to play it safe likely will experience a crop shortage during harvest season.

Third, fear can *polarize* the people it controls. I've observed that individuals under the grip of the lion of fear often withdraw and isolate themselves, missing out on the community they need to succeed in life. Fear is a master isolator; it strives to keep people apart from each other and from what God has in store for them. Fear hinders our involvement in the Kingdom by confining us in a corner where the pain of past hurts and emotions gather. It leaves us feeling alone, disconnected, and paralyzed by doubts. We must resist the grip of fear and break free from its isolating hold, stepping into the light of God's purpose and the warmth of genuine relationships.

I recently spoke with an acquaintance who had been wounded by leadership in the past. Consequently, fear had led this person to a state of withdrawal and polarization, limiting connections to a select few. While this person acknowledged that the reaction to past wounds was misguided, the consequences of fear had lasting effects. While it often takes time to process the challenges we encounter, we should not surrender and refuse assistance from others to aid us in overcoming our fears.

Life moves at the speed of relationships, and it is vital to have people around us who believe in us and in God's plan for our lives. We should never forget that we cannot thrive alone. We need companions who will provide us with the support and motivation we need to move forward. We need friends who will lift us up instead of dragging us down with self-doubt and fear.

Fear does not serve any positive purpose in your life; it is not your friend. It only holds you back from achieving your full potential and living God's abundant life. Fear and faith are mutually exclusive forces that cannot coexist. When fear takes hold, it stifles your trust in God and cancels His plans for you. Conversely, embracing faith releases your worries and anxieties and bolsters your confidence in God's unfailing love and wisdom.

Hebrews 11 beckons us to stroll through the corridors of the faithful, observing those who lived their lives with unwavering faith. The writer emphasized that pleasing God is impossible without faith, and those who approach Him must wholeheartedly believe in God's existence and His rewarding nature for those who seek Him.

Faith is essential for survival; it is an inseparable part of our spiritual life. It forms the core of our ability to triumph over life's challenges and obstacles.

We have the option to determine our approach to every situation that crosses our path—we can confront it with either fear or faith. By choosing faith, we can confidently push forward into the unknown, trusting that God is by our side through every step of the journey. The key to confronting our fears and embracing the fullness of what God has for our life is not taming our fears, but turning our fears around! Conversely, fear offers us an opportunity for growth, a chance to step out in faith, and a reminder that we are on the brink of something extraordinary. Don't let fear hold you back; instead, let it be the catalyst that launches you into the great plans and purpose God has prepared for you. Turn your fears around and step boldly into the adventure that awaits!

Not all fear is detrimental. In the Bible, as in life, we encounter different types of fear. The first one is natural fear. It is an inherent response that emerged in humans after the fall of Adam and Eve. Almost daily, we are bombarded with news about the many natural disasters in our world. For example, living in drought-ridden Southern California

THE LION OF FEAR

for many years, wildfires were a constant concern, especially when the ferocious Santa Ana winds picked up, gusting at speeds up to sixty to seventy miles per hour.

We had to evacuate our home several times due to wildfires approaching dangerously close. It is difficult to fathom the terror that arises when a fire is a mere 150–200 yards from your home, and a police officer is banging on your front door at five in the morning, instructing you to evacuate *now!* The experience fills you with instant fear.

Our home, perched on a hill in the middle of a beautiful avocado orchard, gave us a view of the valley below. I vividly remember looking out one night and watching a fire sweep across the valley below our home. The sight was otherworldly as the fire spread to the orchard near our home, endangering every dwelling in our neighborhood. The fear was indescribable. It was an experience I never wish to face again.

Uncertainties abound in an ever-changing world filled with natural disasters, violence, and political upheavals. As I write this in 2023, we are three years removed from one of the most devastating pandemics in modern history. The pandemic sent shockwaves of fear across the globe, including our community in Southern California. In March 2020, my family and I were pastoring, navigating a turbulent political climate filled with controversy surrounding pandemic management.

As I attempted to lead our congregation during this time, I encountered numerous individuals paralyzed by fear, deeply concerned about the rapid spread of the disease. Many voiced their opinions on how we should handle the situation. Amid the cacophony of voices, I found it challenging to seek God's guidance. Fear attempted to grip my heart amid the rhetoric from city officials, news media, state government agencies, and local medical professionals.

During the height of the pandemic, as we acknowledged the real threat of the virus and took necessary precautions, I recognized a pattern emerging as many allowed fear to infiltrate their minds and hearts, hindering their ability to trust in God for safety.

The impact of COVID-19 was devastating as it claimed the lives of some dear friends, leaving a long-lasting void in our hearts. However, I observed that while fear of the pandemic had a profound effect on specific individuals, it appeared that its impact differed depending on each person's spiritual foundation. Just as COVID-19 was more detrimental to individuals with underlying physical conditions, it held the same implications spiritually. Those without a solid foundation of faith seemed to become even more susceptible to fear's influence, hindering their ability to move forward in faith. Conversely, those with a solid spiritual footing grew stronger in their faith, demonstrating resilience during the challenging times. You can agree or disagree with me, but I firmly believe that fear was like a lion seeking its prey during the pandemic. Unfortunately, many fell victim to its hold and never managed to break free.

When faced with things like hurricanes, tornadoes, or other such dangers, our hearts pound, adrenaline surges, and we instinctively seek safety. Even Jesus experienced this heart-pounding fear as He approached His crucifixion. (See Luke 22:39–46.) Natural fear is real—sometimes almost tangible. But it's a part of the human experience, and it can keep us from harm.

The Bible also speaks of another type of fear—a fear that is spiritual in nature. This fear governs our decisions and steers our path, becoming a repetitive and instinctive response to

THE LION OF FEAR

life's circumstances. This type of fear is a result of the Fall. (See Genesis 3:10.) It is sinful in that it hinders us from trusting and relying on God. Instead, we focus on the troubles surrounding us, diverting our attention from the One who holds universal authority. This type of fear surpasses mere concern for safety and begins to affect people on a spiritual level. It is often described in biblical terms as the "spirit of fear."

An Old Testament example relates to this kind of fear. The people of God, who had been delivered from slavery in Egypt, were on the brink of entering the Promised Land. In Numbers 13 we see a classic illustration of fear overtaking the people of God. When the twelve spies were dispatched to survey the land of Canaan, all but two returned with a fearful account of giants. They were focusing on the giants instead of the grapes. They were looking at the walled cities instead of the valleys that flowed with milk and honey. They should have risen up and yelled, "Let's grab a grape and go! The land is ours for the taking!" Instead, they let fear override their faith, and as a result they spent forty years in the wilderness. All because of fear!

That is the type of fear I'm addressing—the fear that hinders you from stepping into your promised destiny. The fear that erodes your confidence in the person God created you to be. This type of fear prevents you from claiming the promises destined for you since the beginning of time.

During my travels across the nation ministering in various churches and engaging with people of all ages, one prevailing theme emerges: the debilitating impact of fear on people's lives. If this statement resonates with you, you know firsthand how fear can dominate your thoughts and annihilate your potential. But it is time to break free. You have too much potential to stay locked inside the prison of fear. It's time to embrace your destiny, dive into that pit of darkness, and defeat the lion of fear once and for all. I don't want you to be overrun by fear; instead, I want to see you trample fear underfoot as you pursue your calling.

If we use the word "fear" as an acronym, we can discover an important truth for our journey toward success in living for God. There are two approaches when confronting FEAR: (1) Face Everything and Run, or (2) Face Everything and Rise. These two approaches can be likened to the "flight or fight" response. Fear often leads individuals to a critical juncture: either retreat from their potential or rise to the challenge and pursue their calling. I have faith you will choose to rise above, conquer your fears, and embrace the abundant possibilities that await you in God's design for your life.

If you will meditate on the scriptural passages below and allow them to permeate your mind and heart, they will reinforce your identity and purpose as envisioned by God:

> "No weapon formed against you shall prosper, and every tongue which rises against you in judgment you shall condemn. This is the heritage of the servants of the Lord, and their righteousness is from Me," says the Lord. (Isaiah 54:17)

> Fear not, for I am with you; be not dismayed, for I am your God. I will strengthen you, yes, I will help you, I will uphold you with My righteous right hand. (Isaiah 41:10)

> "I will never leave you nor forsake you." So we may boldly say: "The Lord is my helper; I will not fear. What can man do to me?" (Hebrews 13:5–6)

THE LION OF FEAR

For God has not given us a spirit of fear, but of power and of love and of a sound mind. (II Timothy 1:7)

Yea, though I walk through the valley of the shadow of death, I will fear no evil; for You are with me; Your rod and Your staff, they comfort me. (Psalm 23:4)

Be strong and of good courage, do not fear nor be afraid of them; for the LORD your God, He is the One who goes with you. He will not leave you nor forsake you. (Deuteronomy 31:6)

Peace I leave with you, My peace I give to you; not as the world gives do I give to you. Let not your heart be troubled, neither let it be afraid. (John 14:27)

The LORD is my light and my salvation; whom shall I fear? The LORD is the strength of my life; of whom shall I be afraid? (Psalm 27:1)

God is our refuge and strength, a very present help in trouble. Therefore we will not fear, even though the earth be removed, and though the mountains be carried into the midst of the sea; though its waters roar and be troubled, though the mountains shake with its swelling. Selah. (Psalm 46:1–3)

May these verses serve as a reminder that God's immense love and power will equip you to face any fear and overcome any challenge that stands in your way.

As I study the Word of God and consider the stories of men and women of faith, I am struck by their ability to trust God even in the face of seemingly impossible circumstances. These stories and my own personal experience have taught me that faith grows when we overcome challenges and difficulties. Thus, experiencing significant problems is essential for developing and exercising great faith. Understanding how faith operates reveals that problems, trials, and difficulties can be some of the best things that can happen to you. Through faith, I've learned that the magnitude of the problem points to the magnitude of the possibility. The greater the adversity, the greater the potential advantage! In essence, problems give birth to possibilities!

Sir Edmund Hillary, renowned for being the first to conquer Mount Everest, faced numerous failures and setbacks in his attempts to reach the summit. After one of those unsuccessful endeavors, it is said that he gazed at the towering mountain and defiantly raised his fist, exclaiming, "You have defeated me, but I will return, and I will conquer you because you can't grow any bigger, but I can!"

God operates on a currency that transcends the ways of this world. His currency is faith, and its exchange rate always surpasses the value of the valleys in which we find ourselves. Faith becomes essential in our life's quest, and God uses faith as a powerful force to bring about victory in our journey. As the Bible proclaims, "For whatever is born of God

God uses faith as a powerful force to bring about victory in our journey.

THE LION OF FEAR

overcomes the world. And this is the victory that has overcome the world—our faith" (I John 5:4).

Before we move on, I want to take one more step on this journey of faith by looking at the life of Gideon, the judge (Judges 6–8). In his remarkable story, God utilized faith to shatter Gideon's assumptions and bring about profound transformation. If Gideon had relied solely on his assumptions about himself, he never would have witnessed how a mere three hundred men could defeat a vast enemy force.

This is the type of faith that defeats fear. This type of faith looks at multiplied thousands and says, "I am trusting in the God who can do more than I can even ask or imagine." This faith can look a lion in the eye and say, "You will not destroy me! I am more than a conqueror through Jesus Christ!"

Do you desire to conquer the challenges in your life? Do you long to rise above the temptations of your carnal nature that threaten to engulf you? Embrace with unwavering belief that all things are possible with God, dive into the pit where the lion is lurking, and slay him.

Study Questions

1. How does the author describe the nature and influence of the lion of fear throughout the chapter? What are the specific tactics and effects of fear that the author highlights?

2. The chapter mentions different types of fear, such as natural fear (e.g., fear of physical danger) and spiritual fear (e.g., fear that hinders faith). How does the author distinguish between these types of fear, and why is it important to understand this distinction?

3. The author discusses the role of faith in overcoming fear and emphasizes the need to "turn fear into faith." How does faith enable individuals to confront and conquer their fears, and what practical steps does the author suggest for doing so?

6

THE LION OF APATHY

*The slothful man saith, There is a lion without,
I shall be slain in the streets. (Proverbs 22:13, KJV)*

It advances with deliberate slowness, keeping pace with the leisurely gait of its intended victim. It studies its victim, assessing the best way to hinder or even immobilize it. It shows no regard for past accomplishments and aims to divert its target from achieving anything significant in the future.

Apathy is a distinct yet elusive adversary. Its presence can be so heavily veiled that many individuals remain unaware of its influence. It anesthetizes individuals, locking them in a passive condition void of passion and purpose, rendering them incapable of pursuing their mission. It's been said that the world is a dangerous place, not because of the actions of those who commit evil, but because of those who observe and do nothing.

To fully comprehend the concept of apathy, we must first define its nature. Apathy is the absence of excitement, zeal, interest, or even worry. It represents a disregard for the possibilities of life and prevents a person from advancing. In short, it is a nebulous state of indifference.

The ultimate desire of the enemy is to strip away our passion for life, ministry, family, leadership, and the kingdom

THE LION OF APATHY

of God. His primary objective is to steal, kill, and destroy our dreams and faith. We must put on the complete armor of God and resist the pull of the carnal nature that tempts us to coast through life. We possess immense potential, and it would be a shame to remain ensnared in the jaws of a lion determined to hinder our success.

I find great inspiration in the story of the men of Issachar (I Chronicles 12:32). They understood their times and knew exactly what Israel needed to do. Instead of waiting for someone else to take the lead, they showed initiative, took charge, and made a significant impact on their generation. Two hundred chiefs of the tribe of Issachar, as well as the men under their command, came to David and played a significant role in David's rise to power.

In today's world of social media where people showcase their most triumphant moments, it's easy to feel inadequate and think we lack what they have to offer. The fear of breaking free from the pit and distancing ourselves from the lion's influence is frequently heightened by the notion that others are pursuing similar endeavors with apparently greater talent and gifts and success. So we remain immobilized within the lair of apathy, held captive by a sense of insignificance, when in truth we are perfectly positioned to thrive and break free from the lion's grasp.

Escaping the clutches of apathy doesn't require a degree in rocket science or a doctorate in theology; it simply necessitates action. Action is the antidote for apathy. How does one become action-oriented? By getting up and taking that first step.

The prophet Micah reminded us of the proper response to the enemy's assaults when he declared, "Do not rejoice over me, my enemy; when I fall, I will arise; when I sit in darkness, the LORD will be a light to me" (Micah 7:8).

It is important to instill within our spirit a resilient get-up-and-go attitude that defangs and declaws the lion. I've come to realize that attitude truly is everything; it holds the power to shape our course. Allow me a soapbox moment. When I was sixteen or seventeen, I penned this statement in the back of my Bible: *Attitude determines direction, and direction is more important than speed.*

Your attitude is the compass that determines your direction. The speed of your progress is inconsequential because, whether fast or slow, as long as you keep moving you are accomplishing something. Solomon wisely stated, "The race is not to the swift, nor the battle to the strong" (Ecclesiastes 9:11, KJV). Apathy wants you to lose heart and give up before the official fires the starting gun. Remember that the race doesn't belong to the swiftest runner but to the one that endures to the end.

There is more to life than what you presently see and experience. God has a unique purpose vital to this generation that only you can fulfill. Your life holds significance, and it is up to you to fulfill the potential that lies within. You have a mission, and God has equipped you to accomplish it.

The enemy is aware of the immense potential within you. Consequently, he insinuates apathy, indifference, and mediocrity into your mind and spirit. As we progress through this book, we will confront the lion of mediocrity, but suffice it to say the lions of apathy and mediocrity work hand in hand to make you settle for the status quo and imprison you in failures and regrets. As I contemplate the adversary's intent to thwart the impact your life was meant to have, my thoughts turn to Jesus' directive to His disciples as He sent them forth to engage in supernatural ministry. He said, "Behold, I give you the authority to trample on serpents and scorpions, and

THE LION OF APATHY

over all the power of the enemy, and nothing shall by any means hurt you" (Luke 10:19).

Solomon wrote a proverb about a lazy individual who avoids venturing into the streets, fearing a lion might harm him. Those who fear this lion confine themselves to the safety of their surroundings, unaware that it's not the external lion they should fear. The cause for greatest concern lies in the internal lion's resounding roar—the lion of apathy that has trapped and hindered many. Our world doesn't need more sluggards lying around, paralyzed by apathy. Their indifference has caused their faith to shrivel up. Their life is void of the get-up-and-get-after-it spirit.

At times, we let not only the adversary but also the opinions of those around us to induce apathy. We must firmly reject the idea of allowing someone's opinion to divert us from our purposeful journey. They aren't walking in our shoes! They aren't making the same world-changing strides as we are, so why should their opinion hold any weight?

What things hinder you from stepping beyond the threshold of your uncertainties into the realm of potential outside your comfort zone? Have you looked at the challenges ahead and convinced yourself it isn't worth the struggle? Or have you looked at the lion lurking within and made the decision to conquer it regardless of how big, bad, and ugly it appears? The decision is in your hands. A future brimming with potential awaits if you opt to rise from the cushion of comfort and venture onto the path that, though challenging, eventually leads to success.

I assure you the instant you emerge from the abyss of apathy, there will be individuals who will disapprove. Pay them no mind. It's neither worthwhile nor productive to let their opinions impede your progress. There's too much waiting

THE LION OF APATHY

for you ahead to allow the obstacle of other people's opinions to hinder your journey.

Growing up with my two brothers in southern Idaho, we spent much time playing basketball—at least when there wasn't a colossal seventeen feet of snow on the ground. I distinctly recall my junior high days when I tried out for the basketball team and made it. However, I didn't receive much playing time because everyone on the opposing team seemed to know which direction I would dribble.

I can still hear the opposing coach's voice: "See that tall skinny one-handed kid? He's going right!" But their opinions didn't stop me from playing because I had a point to prove. I learned a valuable lesson: someone's opinion of me does not define who I am. In other words, I am not who they say or think I am. The same goes for those who are trying to limit you. You are not who they say you are. Your true worth and potential go far beyond their limited perspectives.

I refuse to confine my life inside the box, restricted by my past failures. I refuse to fall for the deceitful notion that I should be limited by what other people think of me. Those restrictions lead to apathetic living, and, quite frankly, apathetic living is nothing short of pathetic living.

You aren't meant to sit passively by, waiting for someone else to take charge and fulfill what needs to be accomplished. You are called to act upon the callings, gifts, and talents bestowed upon your life. Take a cue from David, Benaiah, Gideon, and Deborah. Ask yourself: Should I allow others to confine me within a box of apathy, or should I break through those limitations and let my destiny unfold before me as God intended?

Allow me to provide some tried-and-true strategies to combat the lion of apathy.

Act

As a baseball enthusiast and former Little League pitcher (watch out, Shohei Ohtani), I learned a fundamental principle of the sport: you cannot reach second base if you keep your foot on first. In other words, progress requires you to step out of your comfort zone and take the necessary steps toward your goals. It's quite profound, isn't it? However, if we're truthful with ourselves, many of us struggle to make progress because we're unsure of how to step beyond the comfort zone that has become our long-standing refuge.

To overcome the lion of apathy in your life, you must act—rise above the limits that have held you back. Embrace forward motion and propel yourself toward success. Progress starts with movement.

What if Benaiah had walked by that pit on that fateful day, shrugged his shoulders, and said, "I don't have time to deal with that lion right now. It's not urgent anyway. It's stuck in that icy pit and can't get out." Can you imagine the havoc that lion would have caused after the ice and snow melted?

Pursue Purpose and Passion

This concept is a double-edged sword of success. Purpose and passion are inseparable. Discover your purpose, the place where you were designed to operate effectively, and pursue it with determination. The passion will naturally follow.

Let me reemphasize: Without purpose, passion falters, and without passion, you may find yourself settling into apathy—no interest, no direction, and no movement. Discover your purpose, and I promise you that your passion will undoubtedly follow.

I challenge you to get out of bed every morning and speak this powerful affirmation into your mind and heart:

"I am filled with purpose and destined for greatness. I am chosen to make a difference in my generation. No weapon, tool, person, or voice formed against me will prosper. I am a child of God, and I am exactly who He says I am. This is my purpose."

Whenever challenges cause doubts about my identity in Christ, I confidently declare these words aloud to myself and the adversary. I want Hell to hear my proclamation.

Make Yourself Available

Availability is paramount. We must dedicate ourselves to being open and receptive to God's work within us. A turned-off water hose cannot impact anything; it yields no flow. We must remain open and available to receive what God has in store for us and embrace life's lessons. Availability is the key to unlocking profound transformations!

Trust the Process

Breaking free from apathy's grip on your life won't happen overnight. It will require time and perseverance, making it one of the most challenging tasks you've ever taken on. Nevertheless, don't give up. The result is entirely worth the effort.

You may find yourself returning to this chapter time and again, and that's okay. Perseverance is key. Trust the process of action, purpose, passion, and availability.

You Must Reach Out for Help

This battle cannot be fought alone. That's why I am grateful you're reading this book. It was meant to support you, to remind you that you are not alone in confronting these lurking lions. To illustrate, allow me to share a personal experience from my college days. While my friends were out playing golf, I found myself idling in the library, attempting to twiddle my thumbs (which I never quite mastered, but I became an expert at giving a "thumb" up). Eventually, I decided to reach out to a buddy of mine and ask him to teach me how to play golf. He obliged and became my golf instructor.

Trust me; watching others play golf would have been far easier than learning to play the game myself. Golf is challenging enough for people with two hands; imagine trying to hit a ball while gripping the driver with only one. During my initial learning phase, getting the ball beyond ten or fifteen yards was a stroke of luck, but eventually, I got the hang of it. Now I can hit the ball over two hundred yards on a good day! Just as perseverance was essential in improving my golf game, the same holds true when combating the lion of apathy. Perseverance is key! Keep at it, and you will triumph over this beast that desires to control you.

Asking for help isn't a sign of weakness; it signifies your recognition that you can't do this on your own. Life can be challenging, and it's easy to lose your way when you face difficulties alone. Having supportive people by your side who offer you guidance along the path that God has chosen for you is essential in reaching your destination.

Consider finding an accountability partner so you can journey together through this book. Challenge each other and witness the transformation unfold as you respond to the study questions. Remember you're not alone in this battle; we are in this together.

You have the power to wage war against this lion of apathy. You just need courage and determination. Don't let a defeat discourage you; the real significance lies in the battle ahead. I firmly believe you possess what it takes to conquer this lion. So rise again and again if you must, and keep press-

THE LION OF APATHY

ing forward! Your promise is within reach, waiting for you to claim it.

Study Questions

1. What are the key characteristics and tactics of the lion of apathy as described in the chapter? Explore how apathy is portrayed as a predatory force in the text and how it affects an individual's life and ambition.

2. How does the concept of "purpose and passion" relate to overcoming apathy? Discuss the connection between having a clear purpose and the enthusiasm or passion required to combat apathy. What steps can individuals take to discover and pursue their purpose?

3. According to the chapter, why is seeking help and support essential in overcoming apathy? Analyze the author's emphasis on reaching out for help and the importance of not fighting the battle against apathy alone. How can individuals find and utilize a support system in their own lives?

7

THE LIONS OF SELF

*For where envy and self-seeking exist,
confusion and every evil thing are there. (James 3:16)*

In this chapter we will examine not just one lion in a pit, but multiple lions that lurk in our innermost being. When self takes center stage in a person's life, the consequences extend far beyond a few close individuals; they reverberate throughout generations.

Through my years of working with others, I've observed the effect that self-centeredness can have on individuals who prioritize their own interests above everyone and everything else. Self-centered people often encounter conflicts in their relationships and tend to react with heightened sensitivity when confronted about their conduct. Additionally, they may grapple with diminished self-esteem, leading to instances where they react negatively to external circumstances even when these situations are unrelated to their own lives.

While it may be natural for individuals to display some degree of selfish behavior, particularly when involved in challenging circumstances, excessive self-absorption can develop into a detrimental habit that undermines one's connections with family members and personal relationships. Self-centered individuals fail to experience personal growth or progress in their lives. After all, they probably believe they have everything figured out, leaving them with little motivation to pursue growth.

We won't discuss all the lions pertaining to self, but we will examine a few so we may better understand the effect these lions can have on our future. The first of these is self-doubt, which can surface when we least expect it.

The Lion of Self-Doubt

I've discovered through experience that self-doubt sabotages more dreams than failure and mistakes combined. Self-doubt acts as the enemy of our faith, an unyielding tyrant determined to keep us enslaved to perceived limitations and inconsistencies. Self-doubt erodes our sense of worth, stifles our ability, and stunts our faith in the people God created us to be.

One potential consequence of self-doubt is a gradual erosion of self-confidence. Pursuing achievements or reaching new heights becomes a fading dream as doubt tightens its chain around our ankles, tethering us to the past or to the perception that we are incapable of overcoming obstacles. This self-imposed limiting habit is exhausting; it drains our vitality and prevents us from stepping into the abundant life that Christ has promised.

During my first year of grade school, a significant incident captured the essence of self-doubt. I was born in the relatively small town of Pendleton, Oregon, and my birth defect quickly garnered public attention among the closely connected residents. One local businessman in the area displayed great kindness by finding a way to induct me into the Shriners. The Shriners are renowned for their hospitals and expertise in working with individuals in need of prosthetics.

THE LIONS OF SELF

The Shriners fitted me with a prosthetic in my preschool years, but I rarely put it on, and my parents never forced me to wear it. When I entered the first grade, I was fitted with what I affectionately called my "hook." I wore it occasionally just to amuse myself by scaring the girls. At that age I was convinced that all girls had cooties.

One day while wearing my hook, a friend and I were playing on the playground, enthusiastically chasing after a red rubber ball. During our jump for the ball, my hook accidentally jabbed him on the lip, causing blood to trickle from the wound. He screamed in pain, but I confess I found it somewhat fascinating. Unfortunately, my first-grade teacher didn't share my excitement. She promptly pulled me aside and scolded me for wearing the hook to school because of its potential danger. I read the conflicted feelings on her face as she attempted to make me understand how different I was.

That incident marked the last time I wore my prosthetic to school. My teacher handed me a sealed envelope addressed to my parents and placed it in my take-home homework folder. Dread filled me as I awaited my father's return from work, fearing I might be in trouble for what had transpired on the playground. When my dad opened the note, he read it quickly, folded it back up, and set it on the counter. Instead of reprimanding me, he lifted me up, embraced me tightly, and spoke words that will resonate in my heart forever. He said, "Darin, you are fearfully and wonderfully made, and God has great things in store for you. You are not defined by what this letter says."

To this day I have no knowledge of the contents of that letter, as my parents never allowed me to see it. Their love and support shielded me from its potential negativity, reinforcing a profound belief in my worth and purpose.

THE LIONS OF SELF

Fast-forward three years to the middle of fourth grade. Our family had moved from Salinas, California, to the quaint farming community of Kimberly in southern Idaho. By the time I arrived, the school year was already in full swing, and friend groups had solidified. I desperately wanted to fit in but found it difficult to do so.

During recess, I attempted to join a game of football, but no one would let me participate because I had only one hand. The rejection devastated me, and as we returned to the classroom after recess, I could no longer hold back my emotions. I collapsed at my desk and sobbed uncontrollably. A fellow student named Chelle Morrill noticed what had happened and promptly informed my fourth-grade teacher about the situation and the reason for my meltdown.

My fourth-grade teacher, Mr. Jenkins, stood in stark contrast to my first-grade teacher. While I can't recall my first-grade teacher's name (I tried to erase it from memory), the memory of Mr. Jenkins remains vivid in my mind. On that day, he did something that left a lasting impact on my heart.

After the class settled down, he started selecting students to come forward and proceeded to point out the positive differences between students. As he continued, my heart raced with fear. Then, to my apprehension, I heard my name called. As a new student from a different state, already struggling with doubts about my worth, I once again found myself in the spotlight, called out by a teacher. However, what happened next completely altered the course of my life. As I walked to the front, visibly shaken in front of my classmates, Mr. Jenkins placed his arm around me and directed their attention to my one good hand. With unwavering confidence, he declared, "Darin is no different than anyone here. This is how he was created, and he can do anything you and I can do."

On that momentous day, any lingering doubt about my identity and worth vanished. Throughout my time in good old Kimberly, Idaho, I held firm to the realization that God doesn't make mistakes. The doubt that could have had a profound effect on me was brilliantly dispelled, thanks to the unwavering support of my parents and teachers like Mr. Jenkins. His example has touched countless lives and continues to inspire others through mediums like this book.

If you ever find yourself doubting who you are, take courage. Remember you are fearfully and wonderfully made by God, who never intended for you to doubt your abilities or worth. Embrace the belief that He has magnificent plans in store for you. Confront that lion of self-doubt with unwavering faith in God. Even if it takes time, rise like Gideon and listen to the voice of God as He affirms that you are a mighty person of valor. Though it might not seem evident at first glance, trust that God sees your true worth and potential. Embrace His words of encouragement and step into the greatness He has destined for you.

The Lion of Self-Centeredness

Self-centeredness is a scourge on our existence, blinding us to the true essence of life, ministry, and service. It transforms every situation into a stage on which self has the starring role. If you are under the control of this lion, you may react negatively if your efforts go unrecognized, become upset when someone else receives credit, and fail to acknowledge the impact of this behavior on others while remaining focused solely on your own grievances.

We are summoned to a higher calling that goes beyond our individual wishes and cravings. The Spirit's purpose within us calls us to dedicate our lives to things that leave a lasting impact and endeavors that will endure beyond our own existence. We are called to labor toward eternal matters rather than for selfish gain. The lion of self-centeredness tempts us to fixate on our reflection in the mirror and focus on our needs and desires rather than gazing out upon a world ripe for positive change and abundant harvest.

Our mission is to be change agents in our world, to labor in a manner that profoundly transforms the lives of others through our actions and the words that guide them toward an abundant life in Jesus Christ.

While I was in graduate school I was introduced to what is known as the Johari Window. The Johari Window is a tool created by psychologists Joseph Luft and Harrington Ingham in 1955.

Johari Window

	Known to self	Not known to self
Known to others	Arena	Blind Spot
Not known to others	Facade	Unknown

THE LIONS OF SELF

This tool aims to enhance people's understanding of their relationships and improve their communication skills while fostering self-awareness. The Johari Window is structured like a windowpane with four quadrants, each symbolizing distinct aspects of self-awareness and interpersonal communication. I believe it also can prompt us to recognize hidden aspects within our hearts and perhaps uncover some elements we may not be aware of. To that end, here are the four quadrants and their defining attributes:

1. *The Open/Arena Area* involves anything you know about yourself and are willing to share with others. There are no secrets here; it is the "this is who I am" window, and everyone knows it.

2. *The Blind Spot Area* refers to aspects of yourself that you are unaware of but that are evident to others. The lion of self-centeredness often hides in this quadrant, as you remain oblivious to these traits, behaviors, or emotions. It's like you're wearing blinders that prevent you from seeing the forest for the trees. Others perceive the trees clearly, but you remain ignorant of their existence.

3. *The Hidden/Facade Area* comprises aspects of yourself that you are aware of but are unwilling to reveal to others. This pane often holds personal secrets or sensitive information you want to keep concealed. You create a facade, putting on a show knowing full well that the lion is lurking just beneath the surface.

4. *The Unknown Area* encompasses aspects unknown to yourself and everyone else except God. This is the sacred domain in which David fervently prayed that his Creator would search the secret places of his heart and reveal the things that were hiding there.

While this window is commonly employed to assess interpersonal awareness and helps us understand how we see ourselves and how others see us, I want to focus our attention on the *hidden/facade area* and establish a biblical framework for our study.

During His ministry, Jesus placed significant emphasis on the core of our existence—the state of our heart. Jesus acknowledged our human tendency to become consumed by self-centeredness. He stressed the importance of evaluating our inner motivations on a daily basis.

We tend to strive for an image that doesn't reflect who we truly are. We wear a mask and often give in to the temptation to believe the entire essence of life revolves around our wants and wishes. This concealed aspect forms a secluded realm within us, constructing a false front that, when under pressure, could crumble, leaving us exposed and susceptible to the grip of the lion.

The Pharisees and Sadducees resided within this arena. Throughout Jesus' ministry, He frequently rebuked them for their obsession with self.

> Woe to you, scribes and Pharisees, hypocrites! For you are like whitewashed tombs which indeed appear beautiful outwardly, but inside are full of dead men's bones and all uncleanness. Even so you also outwardly appear righteous to men, but

inside you are full of hypocrisy and lawlessness. (Matthew 23:27–28)

Why did Jesus display such strong criticism? Why did He confront the prominent religious figures of His time with such intensity? He understood that the inner state of a person's heart, the concealed territory, holds far greater peril than any superficial front we might show.

Jesus was familiar with Solomon's wisdom in Proverbs 4, which advises, "Keep your heart with all diligence, for out of it spring the issues of life" (Proverbs 4:23).

In simpler terms, everything originates from the heart. Jesus later underscored this concept when instructing His disciples on the interpretation of a parable. He stated, "For out of the heart proceed evil thoughts, murders, adulteries, fornications, thefts, false witness, blasphemies" (Matthew 15:19).

This lesson should prompt us to examine our hearts daily, ensuring that any dangers are not buried so deeply that they might emerge one day, overpower us, and wreak havoc on our lives and the lives around us. This responsibility takes precedence over everything else. Be cautious of the self-centered lion within! Make sure your life isn't just about yourself, negating the purpose for which you were placed on this planet.

The Lion of Self-Pity

The lion of self-pity often stems from one's past and cries for sympathy from anyone who will listen. Self-pity is a self-indulgent feeling of unhappiness about oneself and one's problems. These people fall into the pit of thinking they have more problems than anyone else and therefore have suffered more than anyone else.

THE LIONS OF SELF

In this era, the impact of social media is a matter of genuine concern. Don't get me wrong, I'm not against social media in principle; however, I have reservations about its misuse, mainly when we present ourselves in a more positive light than we deserve and seek sympathy from others to avoid facing genuine challenges.

Some people avoid addressing their challenges because they enjoy the attention they gain from others regarding their struggles. This desperate plea stems from a sense of pride, and, if uncontrolled, it has the potential to bring about their downfall. Each of us faces our own set of difficulties, and if we permit them, these issues will dominate us and compel us to gather sympathizers and those who perceive us as mistreated.

This destructive lion of self-pity is associated with emotions like envy, anger, laying blame on others for what they are going through, and occasionally even displaying hostility toward others.

We frequently underestimate the harmful impact on others by dismissing self-pity as mere childishness or immaturity. However, its influence runs far deeper, and it can affect anyone who encounters an individual ensnared in the grip of this beast.

I could have built a house of self-pity based on my circumstances and surrounded myself with people who would pity me. Nevertheless, I chose not to indulge in self-pity. I recognized that God has a grand purpose for my life that extends beyond what might be seen as a drawback. What some might label a disadvantage has morphed into the greatest advantage of my life. I am resolute in not allowing it to define me, for God has given me the authority to shape my life's definition!

THE LIONS OF SELF

The Lion of Self-Righteousness

Concealed from sight, the lion of self-righteousness struts with an air of arrogance. It projects an image far superior to who it truly is. We often perceive this lion as an adorable cub, oblivious to the fact that as it matures, it will distort our perception of genuine righteousness.

This cub of self-righteousness carries a deceitful disposition, promoting a harmful ideology that negatively impacts our personal well-being and influences the people we encounter along life's path. People often remain oblivious to the fact they are ensnared within the jaws of this creature; they display a condescending attitude toward those they perceive as less righteous than they.

In the self-righteous person's quest for validation, they often cause harm. The same pattern can be seen in the story of Satan, who was expelled from Heaven when he arrogantly declared himself mightier than the Almighty. His pride, which served as the underlying foundation of self-righteousness, led to his downfall from heavenly grace.

What is the source of self-righteousness? How does it remain concealed beneath the surface, nestled close to our hearts?

Self-righteous actions frequently arise from feelings of insecurity or inadequacy. When individuals consistently seek to elevate themselves by belittling others, it can indicate a feeling of self-righteousness. This tendency arises perhaps more frequently than we are willing to admit, causing us to look down on the behaviors or lifestyles of others while disregarding our common humanity and our own imperfections while adopting an air of self-righteousness.

Let's face the truth: we often rush to pass judgment when observing the lives of individuals deemed more successful or those who perhaps possess a more influential role or display greater talent. It's curious how criticizing others can make us feel superior while simultaneously distracting us from our own shortcomings. This self-righteous attitude can even lead to feelings of pride.

This lion's presence is evident as it stalks through the pages of the Bible, searching for its next target. We witness its influence in the story of the prophet Jonah, whom God directed to preach repentance to the Ninevites. When they did indeed repent, Jonah's reaction revealed he was caught in this lion's grip. He was upset because God forgave the Ninevites instead of destroying them. Presumably, in his self-righteousness, Jonah thought he knew better than God and resented Him because of His decision to show mercy to Israel's enemy.

Nowhere is this lion more evident than in the account of the Pharisee and the tax collector found in Luke 18. The Pharisee openly boasted of his righteousness before God and proceeded to measure his own righteous stature against that of the humble tax collector, who was so repentant he couldn't even bring himself to lift his gaze. Jesus promptly reinforced the lesson that people who elevate themselves will find themselves brought low, whereas those who embrace humility will ultimately be uplifted.

Self-righteousness shows no partiality. It will target anyone who permits it to take root in their existence. People who are engulfed by self-righteousness frequently become preoccupied with the toothpick in their brother's eye while ignoring the massive beam protruding from their own. I've observed many individuals who hold differing beliefs or opinions in matters that have no eternal consequence, yet they exhibit a harsh or judgmental demeanor toward people they encounter who do not believe as they do or who approach things in a manner different from their own.

I believe self-righteousness arises in people for two main reasons: (1) Some people value their own worth above that of God. This is echoed in Proverbs 21:2, "Every way of a man is right in his own eyes, but the LORD weighs the hearts." (2) There are some who want to showcase their righteousness, much like the Pharisee who compared himself to the tax collector. Jesus approached this point in a straightforward manner in Matthew 6 when He stated, "Take heed that you do not do your charitable deeds before men, to be seen by them. Otherwise you have no reward from your Father in heaven" (Matthew 6:1).

I feel like I'm treading a delicate balance as I record these musings because I don't want to come across as self-righteous when describing those who exhibit such behavior. Nevertheless, I wish to underscore the importance of remaining vigilant against this lion and actively cultivating the righteousness of Christ within our lives. We should strive to progressively embody His essence and detach ourselves from influences and spirits that lead us astray. Our greatest longing should be to embrace the same love Christ exemplifies while realizing there is always room for growth.

The Lion of Self-Perception

Life presents us with many challenges on our journey toward achieving our purpose. Most of these challenges arise from the things we harbor in our hearts. We have tried to identify the areas that hinder our progress and prevent us from achieving the destiny God has planned for us. These challenges, represented by the lions we have encountered, may appear in unique seasons of our lives, and we must fight earnestly to overcome them and experience the victory God has for us.

THE LIONS OF SELF

Defeating lions helps us become the people God created us to be and provides an opportunity for us to draw closer to God and deepen our relationship with Him. It's impossible to draw close to God when a lion is standing between us and the one who created us.

Let me reemphasize my belief in the incredible potential God has uniquely instilled in you. No one else on earth is quite like you, and the purpose woven into your existence is distinct from anyone else in the universe! You are a remarkable creation, fearfully and wonderfully designed, and it's crucial that you always bear this in mind. I'll continue to echo this truth as long as I live because far too many individuals yield to the inner lions that seek to divert them from this profound revelation.

The lion of self-perception has the potential to obstruct us from realizing everything God has promised in our lives. This lion may seem small when viewed within the context of the other lions we've discussed, but it is deceptively ferocious. Our self-perception is intricately tied to how we navigate life, engage with others, and relate with those we consider to be near and dear to us. An unhealthy self-perception and a lack of understanding how much God loves us will keep us from wholeheartedly embracing the Creator's intended purpose for our lives.

What influences our self-perception? I submit that shame is the most harmful emotion emerging from the shadows, and it invariably accompanies this lion of self-perception. Shame could be classified as a lion on its own, yet I've chosen to position it within the realm of perception, for it frequently serves as the accompanying beast that distorts our self-image.

Shame can lead individuals to believe they are undeserving of God's love, the love of others, and even self-love. This is all a result of sin. The Fall had a profound impact on our connection with our Creator. Sin severed this once-unbroken relationship, leading to the suffering caused by sin's consequences. Sin introduced humanity to an entirely unfamiliar emotion on that pivotal day as shame entered the world. Since then, shame has remained a constant presence, ready to pounce on the unwary.

If we are not aware of the impact of shame, it can drive us to engage in actions we never thought we would. Why? Because shame convinces us that we are fundamentally flawed, compelling us to seek refuge from anyone or anything that triggers those feelings. People attempt to cloak the pain of shame by resorting to various false substitutes. They find themselves looking for something to cover the shame, as Adam and Eve did in the Garden. They find themselves doing everything in their power to stifle the resounding shouts of shame, which relentlessly insist they are worthless failures, incapable of achieving anything meaningful, and destined for insignificance.

The beast of shame muddles your perspective on your identity in Christ, leading you to isolate yourself and descend into a pit that was never meant for you. God has a distinct purpose for your life that can break the grip of shame that has ensnared your heart, enabling you to step into the vision of God's divine design for you.

If you regard yourself as unworthy, inadequate, or inferior to others in terms of potential, you will struggle to overcome the beast of shame, leading to a life filled with misery and missed opportunities. If you are experiencing shame from hurts you have carried for years, or if you feel shame from past mistakes, know that the love of the Father can truly heal the pain you carry. Christ gave Himself a sacrifice for you, so acknowledge your worth. Embrace the love of God that has been generously poured into your heart. Love possesses the strength to vanquish the beast of shame and restore your true self-perception!

Study Questions

1. How does self-centeredness affect one's ability to build and maintain meaningful relationships, both personally and professionally?

2. What strategies and practices can individuals employ to identify and overcome self-doubt, preventing it from limiting their personal growth and potential?

3. How can self-pity and self-righteousness negatively impact a person's life, and what are some practical steps to avoid falling into these destructive patterns of thinking and behavior?

8

THE LION OF UNFORGIVENESS

Unforgiveness is a poison that shrivels the heart. It means a person cannot truly live in the present as they're always thinking about the past. – Carolyn Miller

Among all the lions that will be examined within the pages of this book, this cunning lion seems to sow more chaos than its counterparts. The lion of unforgiveness frequently emerges in the aftermath of life's most agonizing experiences: pain stemming from a fractured relationship, subversion orchestrated by a friend or leader, a wound from an unexpected tragedy, or even the venom that surges within one's soul following a violent disagreement with family or friends. Unforgiveness lurks, poised to ambush us at our most vulnerable moments, striking when our hearts are most open and exposed.

Bitterness, envy, and spiritual devastation also arise in the aftermath of encounters with this lion, unleashing chaos upon one's sense of reason. Unforgiveness transcends mere emotion; it operates as an affliction that, when left unattended, can seep into the soul and rob its victims of years of vibrant living.

Injustice is an unavoidable aspect of living. Jesus cautioned that offenses would come, and if we're not vigilant, they can

THE LION OF UNFORGIVENESS

ambush us and bring destruction to our lives. I'm aware this isn't an earthshattering revelation. But it's the truth. Life will subject you to moments that will test your resolve or ensnare you in a whirlwind of unavoidable difficulty, either of which might originate from this lion of unforgiveness.

I have journeyed alongside many who were in the throes of unforgiveness. And I tried to help them reach the other side of the suffering from the kind of wound this lion frequently inflicts. While doing so, I observed two elements that often linger in the hearts of those who refuse to forgive.

First, unforgiveness locks you in the prison of your past. You were not designed to share a cell with the regrets and pains of yesterday. There is no future in the past. If you can't break free from unforgiveness, you'll remain in the prison of past hurts and offenses, serving a needless life sentence.

Second, if unforgiveness is allowed to persist, it will eventually yield a crop of bitterness. The longer bitterness resides in your heart and spirit, the more it will rule your thoughts and eventually mold your character and interactions with other people in your life.

Even as you read these words you may feel a surge of bitterness welling up within you, bringing back memories of times when you were mistreated or offended. Your mind may be flooded by wounds so deep that they cause restless nights and tormented dreams. I've experienced this overwhelming emotion, having gone through a season that was

If unforgiveness is allowed to persist, it will eventually yield a crop of bitterness.

marked by unexpected adversity. On numerous occasions I've grappled with this lion that wanted to consume my potential and sour my spirit. Is it an easy confrontation? Not by any means. But it is imperative to get a fistful of the lion's mane and dispatch the creature before its fangs and claws can inflict irreparable harm on your soul.

The weed of unforgiveness eventually puts down roots of bitterness. The future that once held promise and potential is choked out by roots of bitterness. As the tares of bitterness spread, one is unable to move beyond the hurts and wounds one has suffered. The only way to rid a field of bitterness is to get a spade or a hoe—even an ax or saw if necessary—hack up those roots, and throw them on the burn pile.

Unforgiveness provides an opportunity for the devil to establish a stronghold in our lives. In his letter to the church in Ephesus, Paul urged us not to provide a foothold for the devil (Ephesians 4:27, NLT). Unforgiveness is akin to leaving the door ajar, allowing the devil to insert his foot. Once he has a toehold, it isn't long before he enters and seizes control of our life. We must be constantly aware and refuse to grant him access to our hearts and minds.

People who study lions have observed that bacteria form within lions' mouths and on their claws due to their consumption of carcasses. Some even suggest that the death of an animal or a person that has been bitten or scratched by a lion might not result from the bite or the scratch but rather from the transmission of bacteria into the wound.

We must be careful not to let another person's bitterness infiltrate our inner selves, leading us to get involved in someone else's conflict. In recent years, I've observed individuals taking up the sword of someone else's injustice and wielding it as if it were their own, attempting to champion a cause that has no direct connection to them. Unfortunately, they soon find themselves locked in a cell of bitterness with the person

THE LION OF UNFORGIVENESS

they were trying to champion, and they both suffer spiritual deterioration.

This phenomenon is prevalent in today's social-media-dominated world, where we often engage in battles we have no business fighting. We already have enough of our own internal battles to contend with; we don't need to let someone else recruit us into their fight. No one else's struggle is worth sacrificing one's own soul.

As I mentioned earlier, there have been instances in my personal journey when I needed to work through my own wounds to avoid the infection of bitterness. During these times, it seemed as though I was battling a fever raging in my heart, soul, and mind.

I recall a particular day during prayer when I grappled with the infectious fangs of bitterness that were trying to take hold of my soul. I sensed a prompting from the Lord: "You must learn to work through your wounds." This led me to seek further understanding, and I believe the Lord granted me some illumination. We so often desire swift resolutions, dismissing time as a needless investment. However, from that prayer session, I gathered that the wounds life imposes on us require a deliberate approach to healing, ultimately enabling us to release the burden through the act of forgiveness, all of which takes time. It's often said that time has the power to heal all wounds, so we must ultimately allow the passage of time to have the last word.

Yielding to bitterness often appears more convenient than exerting the effort to forgive. Forgiveness demands painstaking work as you gradually peel away layer after layer of offense, but the positive outcomes outweigh the hard work. If Benaiah had avoided confronting the lion that day, one can only imagine the potential problem it might have caused in the long run. This symbolic lion of unforgiveness has the

THE LION OF UNFORGIVENESS

capacity to leap from one generation to the next, tragically dismantling the lives of those we love and hold dear.

Many books have been written emphasizing the necessity of forgiveness and the journey people travel beyond the injury that has deeply affected their spirit. Jesus cautioned us about the certainty of offenses and encouraged us to navigate through these hurts, emerging on the other side as better individuals, free from the taint of bitterness.

Martin Luther King Jr. has been quoted as saying, "Forgiveness is not an occasional act; it is a constant attitude." The attitude of forgiveness is a powerful tool that can reshape our lives and create a different future. It represents conscious decisions to release resentment, anger, and bitterness, liberating us from the weight of anguish and hardship. While forgiveness cannot change the past, it possesses the potential to impact and alter our future.

The attitude of forgiveness can eventually replace bitterness with love, joy, peace, gentleness, goodness, faith, meekness, and self-control. Why would anyone choose to remain locked up in the barren prison of their past? Why would anyone choose a life burdened by bitterness, which will inevitably damage every relationship they hold dear? I urge you to choose forgiveness.

To forgive is to unlock the prison door and release the prisoner. It's to inscribe "Nothing owed" in bold letters across a debt. It's like pounding the gavel in a courtroom and proclaiming, "Not guilty!" It's like gathering up all the trash and disposing of it, leaving the house clean and fresh. Forgiveness is about releasing the grip on our opponents and granting them freedom, regardless of their actions.

So I encourage you to confront this deceptive lion before it inflicts harm upon you, your marriage, your children, or your future. Act immediately! Initiate that phone call, send that letter, write that text message, or arrange a coffee meeting. Embrace forgiveness and experience freedom from the grip of the fangs that have sought to drag you down. Life is too short, and eternity is too long!

Study Questions

1. How does unforgiveness serve as a self-inflicted poison, preventing individuals from fully embracing the present and keeping them locked in the past?

2. How can unforgiveness blossom into bitterness over time, and what are the long-term effects of bitterness on a person's character and relationships?

3. In what ways does unforgiveness grant an opportunity for negativity, spiritual decay, and the influence of the devil in one's life?

4. How can individuals guard against taking up someone else's battles and avoid the infection of bitterness from external conflicts?

9

THE LION OF COMPARISON

Comparison is the thief of joy. — *Theodore Roosevelt*

Even if you spend only a short amount of time on social media, you'll soon feel pressure beginning to mount. It's like an out-of-control monster eager to devour your time and influence your perspective. However, your destiny was never intended to be overshadowed by the lives of others, nor were you designed to sag beneath the weight of their actions or the facade they present in the cyberworld. You face a significant danger when you view the embellished highlight reels of people's lives on social media platforms like Instagram, Facebook, or TikTok. They can make you feel inadequate about your own life's journey.

The peril of comparison is not confined solely to students or young adults; its reach extends to individuals of all ages. Leaders, parents, pastors, and even community figures can fall victim to the wide swipe of this lion's paw. The impact of comparison is far-reaching and causes considerable harm, a reality that carries weight beyond mere amusement.

Thirty to forty years ago this wasn't an issue. Certainly, the lion of comparison has always existed, but within our contemporary society, where real-time news reports are

THE LION OF COMPARISON

instantly accessible, comparison has morphed into an imposing beast of enormous size.

We don't have to delve too deep into the Bible's pages to uncover this destructive force. In Genesis 4 we encounter the story of the first murder in Scripture, when Cain fell prey to this lurking lion of comparison. Let's eavesdrop on the conversation between God and Cain, where the underlying motive for Cain's jealousy was laid bare:

> So the LORD said to Cain, "Why are you angry? And why has your countenance fallen? If you do well, will you not be accepted? And if you do not do well, sin lies at the door. And its desire is for you, but you should rule over it." (Genesis 4:6–7)

The symbolism takes on added significance when we perceive God's message to Cain (paraphrased here): "Choose the righteous path, and you'll thrive. Everything will be great! However, should you turn toward wrongdoing, Cain, picture a lurking lion right outside that door, poised to pounce on you. But here's the crux: it doesn't have to end that way. You possess the ability and the authority to rule over that lion."

The lion of comparison appears to do the most harm in the area of relationships. When we compare ourselves to others, we unwittingly unravel the ties that bind friendships and connections together, often leading to tearing others down. Consider again Cain and Abel. Cain's internal dialogue likely centered on the notion that eliminating his brother would spare him from the constant reminder of his own shortcomings. This echoes the essence of sin—missing the mark.

It is undeniable that comparison can be detrimental to relationships. It leads to feelings of inadequacy and may cause us to view ourselves as less attractive, less gifted, less skilled,

THE LION OF COMPARISON

and less talented than someone else. As a result, we may start to undermine others by scrutinizing their every move on social media, believing that we deserve the same level of attention.

Pew Research conducted a recent survey concerning the influence of social media on today's average teenager. The results were striking.

> When it comes to negative experiences, 38% of teens say that what they see on social media makes them feel overwhelmed because of all the drama. Roughly three-in-ten say it makes them feel like their friends are leaving them out of things (31%) or feel pressure to post content that will get lots of comments or likes (29%). And 23% say that what they see on social media makes them feel worse about their own life. (Pew Research, "Teens and Social Media: Key Findings from Pew Research Center Surveys," April 24, 2023.)

In my teenage years (back in the Jurassic Era), social media wasn't a thing. We didn't have to deal with the negativity that often arises from it. Unlike the current generation, we weren't constantly aware of our friends' whereabouts, so we didn't know if we had been excluded from any events or gatherings.

In a world where social media often promotes misleading information, addressing the pressure to conform to false narratives is crucial. Such pressure can impede individuals from pursuing their God-ordained life purpose, pushing them further into the pit where the ravenous beast of comparison threatens their well-being.

THE LION OF COMPARISON

Let me emphasize the point that a post shared online is a skewed depiction of reality! The quantity of hearts, likes, stars, or thumbs-up does not dictate the worth of one's identity. Our purpose goes beyond the recognition we receive through social media posts.

Two other instances in Scripture that highlight the sin of comparison are found in the tales of two brothers and two sisters who grappled with comparisons.

First, two twin sons came of age in a family environment in which the household dynamic was far from harmonious. One son found favor in his mother's eyes, while the other son basked in the light of his father's affection. The boys' names were Esau and Jacob. Esau was born only seconds before Jacob. The biblical account reveals a significant detail about the twins' birth: when Jacob emerged into the world, he was clinging to his older brother's heel.

This moment laid the foundation for the unfolding narrative of sibling rivalry. Assisted by his mother, Rebekah, Jacob embarked on a journey of comparison with his brother, who was entitled to the birthright by virtue of his status as firstborn. Jacob's desire for his brother's birthright and blessing became all-consuming, driving him and his mother to devise a plan to obtain them.

We must remain vigilant against the grasp of the lion of comparison. The risk stems from the mistaken notion that we should be like others or possess what others have. When we adopt the yardstick of comparison as our measurement, the threats of jealousy, envy, and greed loom large. Consider, for example, the doubts that emerge regarding someone else's successes, which might lead us to scrutinize their spiritual and numerical progress within their leadership or church context. Once the lion of comparison takes hold, we presume their advancement stems solely from compromise. Consequently,

THE LION OF COMPARISON

we begin to question why our growth does not mirror theirs or why we are not being recognized for what we are currently building or experiencing.

Through cunning manipulation, Jacob managed to wrestle the birthright away from Esau, and later he secured his father's blessing through deception. The devious lion of comparison had Jacob's spirit in its grip, driving him to such lengths that he now had to flee from his brother's murderous revenge. Two moments of succumbing to the lion of comparison caused a division within the family, a division that stretched across decades and over centuries.

The presence of this lion and its "pride" of envy and jealousy is not confined solely to the lives of Jacob and Esau. It also figured prominently in the narrative of two sisters, Leah and Rachel. Each of these sisters coveted what the other appeared to possess. Leah yearned for the affection and regard of her husband, which Rachel enjoyed, while Rachel longed to bear children like Leah, whose fertile womb produced six sons and a daughter.

We have previously written about comparison in the lives of Saul and David, but it merits another mention here. David's rising popularity and the resounding praises sung of his triumphs that surpassed those of Saul compelled Saul to compare their achievements. This comparison drove Saul to the brink of madness in seeking to take the life of David and annihilate the perceived threat to Saul's monarchy.

Comparison possesses the power to steer you toward actions you normally wouldn't contemplate in your journey of life and leadership. Refuse to let this prowling lion dictate your choice and path. Subdue this force so you can genuinely rejoice with others, even when their blessings appear more abundant than yours. There's wisdom in acknowledging that we should publicly celebrate those things we might feel privately threatened by.

We must never allow comparison to dismantle our destiny. Let's recognize the value of others in our lives and how we are called to work together to make a difference in our world. It is impossible to defeat a common enemy if we are more at war with each other than we are with the beast that is trying to delay and distract us. May we never fall prey to this predator and let it incite us into dismantling one another rather than fostering unity. Let us triumph over this beast of comparison and advance victoriously together.

Study Questions

1. How does today's pervasive comparison trend, mainly through social media, impact the self-worth and well-being of individuals?

2. In what ways does the act of comparison, as exemplified in the biblical narratives of Cain and Abel, Jacob and Esau, and Leah and Rachel, lead to division and conflict in families and communities?

3. How can individuals avoid falling into the trap of comparison and its destructive consequences?

4. How can one overcome the lion of comparison to genuinely celebrate the successes and blessings of others, even when they seem to surpass one's own achievements?

10

THE LION OF MEDIOCRITY

So then, because you are lukewarm, and neither cold nor hot, I will vomit you out of My mouth. (Revelation 3:16)

The lion of mediocrity, synonymous with the concept of "average," shares many of the same traits as the lion of apathy discussed in chapter 6. They are from the same pride.

Earlier, I recounted an incident from my younger years involving my first-grade teacher and the invaluable lesson my parents instilled within me during those impressionable days. That lesson, along with the revelation of a person's fundamental worth articulated in Psalm 139:14, have been guiding principles in my life for many years. While revisiting this passage a few years ago, I was struck by the words of the psalmist as he prayed to God, affirming that everyone is fearfully and wonderfully made. I sensed a divine impression, a poignant reminder that nobody enters this world as an ordinary being. In other words, *nobody is born average!*

As I engaged in prayer over this verse of Scripture, the inner revelation surged with increasing intensity, eventually solidifying into a life-defining message I have imparted to countless individuals throughout the past several decades. Within each of us resides innate potential and boundless promise. These gifts are woven into our spirit by God, yet we

THE LION OF MEDIOCRITY

often find ourselves settling in the land of Average and establishing residence in the town of Mediocrity, all the while failing to recognize our capacity for so much more.

Life's trials, setbacks, pains, and disillusionments frequently cause many to retreat from the person God has designed them to be and the mission He has called them to accomplish. Consequently, the allure of average becomes a cozy comfort zone, inhibiting them from venturing beyond its borders.

I'll speak candidly: it would have been much easier for me to avoid the challenges I met in my pursuit of success. I could have skidded to a halt at the outer edge of my perceived limitations. I could have opted to remain in a comfortable state of mediocrity, refraining from pushing the boundaries of my potential. I had a whole bagful of excuses at my disposal, and no one would have blamed me.

Winston Churchill said, "To each, there comes in their lifetime a special moment when they are figuratively tapped on the shoulder and offered the chance to do a very special thing, unique to them and fitted to their talents. What a tragedy if that moment finds them unprepared or unqualified for that which could have been their finest hour." This exceptional leader encountered numerous obstacles while journeying toward a position of influence and significance. He endured several disappointing years as a young student. At one point his housemaster reported to his father, "Winston ought to have been at the top of his form, but he was at the bottom." Some have speculated that the boy suffered from dyslexia or ADHD. As he grew into manhood, he contended with mood swings and depression, a condition that ran in the family. However, he eventually learned to harness his boundless energy and became a fearless leader who inspired a nation to win victory for the free world.

THE LION OF MEDIOCRITY

Have you found yourself obstructed by the presence of a lackluster lion deterring you from breaking out of the rut and fully embracing your defining moment of purpose? It seems much easier to let life pass you by, to avoid the challenges that commitment to growth demands. However, a life marked by mediocrity can be equally daunting when the realization dawns upon you that you've been handed a divine summons to rise and confront the lion. Don't be defeated by this adversary. Break out of the rut and secure victory for yourself and for future generations.

I believe that purpose has a pulse. Sometimes it beats quietly, yet it remains a constant reminder of the rhythm of the life you are destined to lead. As your journey unfolds, this heartbeat often gains intensity, growing louder as you draw nearer to the path God has designated for you.

Once you discover your calling, resist the lie that you are average.

Once you discover your calling, resist the lie that you are average—formed out of ordinary cloth. That you can't achieve much because you come from an unremarkable family. You must steadfastly combat the temptation to accept the humdrum existence that countless others have accepted. Regardless of whether it stems from your family, your social circle (or the absence thereof), your mandate is to rise beyond the realm of average and acknowledge the incredible potential your life embodies.

Mark Twain once spoke of an acquaintance, saying, "He died at thirty; they buried him at sixty," implying that the man stopped truly living long before his physical demise. Could it have been the lion of mediocrity that caused this man to forsake a vibrant existence long before he departed from this life? What events transpired in his journey that prompted him to relinquish hope and forsake the pursuit of a rich and fulfilling life? You might not be able to name all the factors that contributed to his decline, but you can be determined to prevent a similar fate from happening in your life.

The enemy recognizes your potential, so he fights against you. If you roll over and play dead, you'll miss out on life's extraordinary adventure. The Bible affirms the truth that you are of great value: "Greater is he that is in you than he that is in the world." Therefore, settling for anything less than what you were created to be and remaining indifferent about your future and success would be wasting the precious gift of life.

What is it exactly that pulls a person into the abyss of the average? Does it stem from birth, genetic composition, or a lack of societal privilege? While some of these as well as other factors may lead a person to settle for mediocrity, two core areas significantly contribute to this condition.

Your Past

Toward the beginning of this chapter I emphasized that everyone is fearfully and wonderfully made and is endowed with potential and promise. Unfortunately, potential and promise sometimes diminish as we navigate life's trials and tribulations.

In our childhood, we embrace dreams of our potential, but as we wend our way along the course of life, those dreams tend to slip away like toy boats caught in the current. They disappear around the bend in the river, leaving us empty and unsure of our identity and direction. Frequently, what takes the place of those dreams and aspirations is a sense of inadequacy, and we permit the very obstacles that wrested our dreams away to shape our perspective for the years ahead.

Your past doesn't dictate your future. The shattered dreams strewn along the watercourse of your purpose do not define your life's essence. The pain, unaddressed struggles, conflicts, and disillusionment do not have the power to determine your triumphs. What transpired in your history remains precisely that—history. It's in the past. Concluded. Finalized. Gather your belongings, bid the past farewell, and take the first step toward the place where God intends for you to reside. Remember everyone carries baggage from the past that, if permitted, could hinder them from breaking out of the rut. The jaws of juvenile blunders and the missteps of midlife can be loosed from your spirit if you will embrace the words God spoke to Jeremiah and recognize that they apply to you as well:

> "For I know the plans I have for you," declares the LORD, "plans to prosper you and not to harm you, plans to give you hope and a future." (Jeremiah 29:11, NIV)

Your past, no matter how dismal it may appear, cannot hinder you from receiving the above word from God into your life. If you genuinely desire to see His purposes unfold within you, then take control of your mindset. Believe you serve a God who is bigger than all the mess and mistakes of yesterday. Believe He has crafted a unique plan for you.

Your Peers

The timeless saying proclaims, "Show me your friends, and I will show you your future." This sentiment is true on many levels. Our peers possess the ability to exert influence, often unintentionally, and steer us toward a state of mediocrity. We can "catch" their lack of aspiration for higher ideals and fall in step with them on the pathway of the average until we find ourselves confined within the boundaries of limited perceptions and squashed dreams.

The psalmist expressed this concept in the first song of the Psalter. Listen in on his advice:

> Blessed is the man who walks not in the counsel of the ungodly, nor stands in the path of sinners, nor sits in the seat of the scornful; but his delight is in the law of the Lord, and in His law he meditates day and night. He shall be like a tree planted by the rivers of water, that brings forth its fruit in its season, whose leaf also shall not wither; and whatever he does shall prosper. (Psalm 1:1–3)

Observe the posture of those who decide to traverse the path alongside those uninterested in pursuing meaningful lives. Initially, they start their journey with a sense of forward movement that propels them in a particular direction. However, as time passes, they stop, stand in place, and permit the influence of the uninspired to insinuate its effects. Almost before they realize it, they find themselves harboring cynicism and indifference.

Conversely, the individuals who continue striding toward their preordained destination end up like trees firmly rooted by the river, producing fruit in due season. They remain steadfast, untouched by idleness as life unfolds around them, thriving and flourishing in every endeavor they undertake. They are the blessed ones!

We must not permit the prevailing norms of our companions to shape our destiny. Numerous lives have crumbled due to the influence of peers who urged them to settle for the status quo instead of striving for success.

You don't have to fall into this trap. You don't have to settle for being an average father focused solely on your career as

THE LION OF MEDIOCRITY

you neglect the difference you could make in your children's lives during their formative years. You don't have to become a mediocre mother, merely existing without imparting influence and impacting your children's lives. Your marriage need not lack passion and fulfillment. You don't have to be a teenager struggling with your identity, allowing your past failures or the pressure of your peers to define you.

Identify the lion of mediocrity and the tactics it employs to ensnare you unexpectedly, confining you to a pit of uninspired existence. You possess immense value and have many contributions to offer. Rise from the couch of complacency and strive to reach your fullest potential.

Study Questions

1. How does the author's personal experience, including his physical limitations and unique circumstances, provide a powerful example of resisting mediocrity and embracing one's potential?

2. This chapter points out that your past and the influence of your peers can contribute to your settling for mediocrity. Can you think of personal experiences or instances where these factors have influenced your choices and aspirations?

3. The author emphasizes the importance of recognizing and defying the "lion of mediocrity." What practical steps can individuals take to confront this adversary in their own lives and fully embrace their potential and purpose?

11

THE LION OF ENTITLEMENT

I'm here today to warn you: I want you to watch out for the adversary. Guard yourself from any spirit of entitlement. Restrain any and all subtle temptation to gain attention or to find ways to promote yourself. – Charles Swindoll

Benaiah's example established a fundamental principle emphasizing the importance of addressing the hidden challenges that lurk beneath the surface. Benaiah's battle with the lion wasn't for sport. He wasn't planning to stuff the lion's head and mount it on the wall or tan the hide for a fireplace rug. His purpose went beyond personal enjoyment; he was fighting to safeguard future generations, ensuring that the predator would never claim another victim. His display of courage serves as a powerful illustration of the requirements needed to establish a legacy that will be recounted for years. It demands our undivided focus if we are to lead purposeful lives, realize our intended potential, and leave a legacy.

Unfortunately, amid the ranks of those who surmounted the obstacles in their path, there are individuals who let such opportunities slip through their fingers. Saul is among them. In our previous discussion of Saul's life we didn't identify every lion that led to his demise, but it's evident that the enemy of entitlement played a significant role. Before we continue, we should establish a clear definition of what entitlement really is.

Entitlement is the belief that we deserve privileges and special treatment. It's a mindset that says, "I should have that even if I haven't truly earned it, because . . . well . . . I'm me!" Entitlement is the belief that we are superior to others, often without concrete evidence to support such a claim. It is the conviction that we are exempt from the rules others are expected to follow.

While Saul is a classic example of someone caught in the jaws of this lion, he is not the only biblical example. For instance, Samson was destined to become a leader of God's people even before he was conceived. His story begins in Judges 13 with a remarkable occurrence in the life of Manoah's wife, Samson's mother. Despite this good woman's barrenness, a visitation from the angel of the Lord imparted a prophecy that instilled in her the faith to anticipate the birth of a son.

Let's look at the unique parameters surrounding the conditions of Samson's birth and life. The parents were instructed to ensure the boy lived according to the Nazirite vow (Numbers 6). An individual undertaking the Nazirite vow was required to adhere to a specific code of conduct, which included refraining from consuming wine, strong alcoholic beverages, and any grape-derived products; letting their hair remain uncut throughout the entirety of the vow; and avoiding physical contact with corpses, including those of immediate family members, unless the individual unintentionally incurred ritual impurity.

Knowing these guidelines helps us grasp the significance of Samson's role. He was no ordinary Israelite; God had chosen and empowered him to liberate the nation from Philistine domination. He was the chosen instrument of God for that

THE LION OF ENTITLEMENT

specific moment! Yet, as time passed, Samson appears to have exploited his position, leading to unfortunate consequences.

The Scriptures chronicle Samson's gradual descent, possibly driven by a sense of entitlement and exemption from rules based on his perceived strengths and commitments. This perspective gradually drew him into a downward spiral.

In our first glimpse of this trajectory of tragedy in Samson's life, we find him on his way to take a bride from the Philistines despite his parents' apprehension and warning. Samson dismissed their reservations about marrying a girl from among the enemies he was destined to subdue. While God eventually used this misguided choice to accomplish His purpose, the narrative is filled with valuable lessons for our understanding.

On his journey to wed this Philistine woman, Samson was passing through the vineyards of Timnah when a roaring lion leaped into his pathway. Samson seized the lion and tore it limb from limb. While this may appear brave and commendable at first glance, his presence in the vineyards raises questions. Samson was prohibited from contact with or partaking of any products of the vine. Why was he "flirting" with something God explicitly commanded him to avoid? Did he consider himself exempt from the terms that bound other Nazirites? Did he discount the boundaries set for his mother, who had accepted the Nazirite restrictions so he could become the mighty liberator of Israel from foreign oppression?

While Samson's motives at this moment in his life remain uncertain, it is evident he was embarking on a precarious path. Subsequently, he crossed yet another boundary by revisiting the vineyards and venturing near the lion's remains. He discovered a cache of honey inside the carcass, reached

THE LION OF ENTITLEMENT

into the cavity, retrieved a handful of honeycomb, and went on his way eating the honey.

What strikes me as both interesting and alarming is Samson's return to a lifeless lion in search of something sweet. Although Samson was prohibited from contact with the dead, we witness him defying this restriction by putting his eager hands into the lifeless lion's remains. This event underscores the danger that lies in unrestrained desires that operate beyond the bounds of divine control. We should be cautious not to revisit the lions we've conquered, under the impression that we can extract something delightful from their demise.

Samson's actions placed him in an increasingly compromised situation. Again, he possibly viewed the rules as irrelevant to his circumstances. He saw himself as exceptional and exempt from the behaviors expected of those chosen by God for significant tasks. This sense of entitlement eventually led to the tragic decision that led to his untimely demise.

Here is the issue that Samson's story presents: individuals ensnared by the lion of entitlement perceive themselves as elevated above the level of their peers. In today's world, unlike any previous era, we observe this phenomenon emerging, whether driven by a generation with limited exposure to the word *no*, or by a culture of indulgence that nurtures a sense of entitlement based on one's perceived self-importance.

In his book *The Challenge of Faith, Walking with God through Pain and Suffering,* Timothy Keller states, "The presumption of spiritual entitlement dooms its bearers to a life of confusion when things in life inevitably go wrong." While entitlement extends its influence beyond the spiritual domain and into the physical realm, this quote holds much truth.

A sense of entitlement can prevent you from realizing your full potential. True strength and purpose emerge from life's struggles and challenges. Your character is shaped, and

THE LION OF ENTITLEMENT

your calling is discovered through these experiences. If you believe that difficulties are unnecessary because of your status or background, you may be hindering yourself from fulfilling the potential that was designed for you by God.

This truth becomes particularly evident in Paul's revelation about the thorn in his flesh—the weakness that surprisingly revealed his greatest strength. This realization has profoundly impacted my own journey. Many have seen the circumstances of my birth as a disadvantage, a weakness. However, it has been my most significant advantage and source of strength, as it has taught me the profound importance of relying on God in every challenge that life presents. Paul said it best.

True strength and purpose emerge from life's struggles and challenges.

> And lest I should be exalted above measure by the abundance of the revelations, a thorn in the flesh was given to me, a messenger of Satan to buffet me, lest I be exalted above measure. Concerning this thing I pleaded with the Lord three times that it might depart from me. And He said to me, "My grace is sufficient for you, for My strength is made perfect in weakness." Therefore most gladly I will rather boast in my infirmities, that the power of Christ may rest upon me. Therefore I take pleasure in infirmities, in reproaches, in needs, in persecutions, in distresses, for Christ's sake. For when I am weak, then I am strong. (II Corinthians 12:7–10)

THE LION OF ENTITLEMENT

Even the apostle Paul recognized the significance of vulnerability and embracing one's shortcomings. Considering this, who are we to presume we are exempt from such experiences and entitled to preferential treatment? The adversary has persuaded certain people that they hold a higher status than others, leading them to believe they should be treated delicately to avoid any form of discomfort or hardship. To truly excel in God's purpose, we cannot assume we have reached a destination or deserve recognition solely due to who our parents are, our social standing, or our past achievements.

Let us remain strong in preventing a sense of entitlement from taking root within us. It is God who raises us up, not our own striving for titles or positions. If we find ourselves thinking that we deserve more, we must shift our attention away from ourselves and toward our Creator. It is important to understand that success and advancement are determined by God. He is the one who raises up and casts down.

I confess that I am not immune to a sense of entitlement. I must continually maintain a sense of gratitude and awareness that God is not indebted to me in any way. It is through His tender mercies and grace that my sins have been forgiven. His blood has cleansed my heart and attitude. God observes the path we walk, and His purpose is for us to be molded into His likeness. We cannot undergo this transformation into His image if our focus remains solely on ourselves, our needs, our desires, and our own way.

Before shifting our focus to another destructive force targeting our futures, it is essential to emphasize that *service* is the antidote to the spirit of entitlement. As Jesus reminded us in Matthew 23:11–12, "He who is greatest among you shall be your servant. And whoever exalts himself will be humbled, and he who humbles himself will be exalted."

THE LION OF ENTITLEMENT

If you find yourself overwhelmed by the spirit of entitlement, immerse yourself in service to others. Adopt an attitude that no task is beneath you in the kingdom of God. Get actively engaged—pick up a shovel, give an offering, go on a missions trip, lead a Bible study, converse with the elderly at a nursing home, volunteer at a soup kitchen, or become involved in your local community, especially with those less fortunate than you. Take action that revolves around aiding and caring for people. The path to breaking free from the grip of entitlement is through humble service to others.

Study Questions

1. This chapter highlights the destructive nature of entitlement and its potential to hinder one's personal and spiritual growth. Can you recall instances in your own life or in the lives of those you know where entitlement has had a negative impact on their journey or relationships?

2. The author mentions the importance of service as an antidote to the spirit of entitlement. In what ways have acts of service and humility helped you or others overcome entitlement and led you to experience personal transformation?

3. The story of Samson's life is used as an example of someone who may have fallen into the trap of entitlement. How can we learn from his experiences and avoid the pitfalls of entitlement in our own lives, striving to remain humble and focused on God's will?

12

THE LION OF LOOKING BACK

But Jesus said to him, "No one, having put his hand to the plow, and looking back, is fit for the kingdom of God." (Luke 9:62)

Many examples from the Word of God encourage and guide us as we keep moving toward the prize. When we examine faith heroes such as Abraham, we can see our Creator leading us toward the future, encouraging us to leave stagnation behind. Abraham's every stride represented a step toward God's promises for him and his family. Was his journey effortless? No. Did Abraham make some painful errors that had consequences for his future? Yes. However, this depiction of Abraham's life underscores a crucial message for us: God desires us to gaze beyond the present and peer into the potential of what is out there for us on the horizon.

This is why we must confront the lion called looking back. The adversary understands we have a future, and God has extraordinary promises in store for us, for our children, and for generations to come. If our enemy can persuade us to turn our sights back toward the place from which God liberated us, he knows he can sabotage our future.

As I pondered this lion that causes many to look back, my mind traveled to the mountains of Washington State and the story of the conversion of my grandparents, Sidney and Ruby

Sargent. My grandfather, affectionately known as Sid, and his high school sweetheart, Ruby, were a beloved and well-liked young couple in the quaint town of Morton, Washington. Sid worked as a logger in the surrounding mountain ranges. He was far from God, having no relationship with the Lord whatsoever.

This occurred during a time when loggers used crosscut saws that required the coordinated efforts of two men. Sid's partner was a fellow named Jess Wills. Together they toiled under the scorching sun, cutting down trees in the Cascade Mountains.

Every day, Jess would share the message of Jesus with Sid, emphasizing how Jesus had the power to transform his life. Sid, who struggled with smoking and drinking, would become furious when Jess talked about how God could remove his cravings for those habits. Sid continuously unleashed a string of curses at Jess, but the man persisted in his efforts to share the gospel message and extend church invitations. One day during a break, Sid walked off to a secluded area holding a cigarette in his hand. As he stood there smoking, he looked up at the sky and said, "God, if you are real, remove the craving for smoking and drinking from my life." He brought the cigarette to his lips for another puff, but it nauseated him. From that moment on, he never smoked again. Returning to the work area, he informed Jess that he would accompany him to church for no reason other than to finally get Jess off his back.

Not long after that, Sid visited the small Pentecostal church in Morton, and there a profound transformation took place in his life. He would often recount the night he met God and received the powerful gift of the Holy Spirit. Following this divine encounter, Sid became a devoted member of the Pentecostal congregation, and he persistently urged

THE LION OF LOOKING BACK

Ruby to join him in attending church or a revival service. Regrettably, she consistently declined. Things escalated to a critical juncture when Sid returned home from work one day to find Ruby waiting by the front door with her bags packed. When Sid walked in, she made it clear to him that she was returning to her father's farm located just outside of town. Sid pleaded with her to stay. He explained how God had transformed his life and made it impossible for him to return to his previous ways. He fervently conveyed that God had the power to bring about a similar transformation in her life if she would go with him to church. However, Ruby remained resolute. While loading the car, Sid offered a silent prayer, imploring God to touch his wife's heart. Together, they set out on the brief journey to Ruby's parents' farm.

As they drove down the dusty road, Sid kept asking Ruby to have a change of heart. All of a sudden she exclaimed, "Stop the car, Sid! All right. I'll go to church with you *one time.*" Well, the rest is history as Ruby experienced the same transformative power of God at work in her life. Together, they assisted in churches across the Northwest, worked in a Bible college in Portland, Oregon, took missions trips around the world, and raised a family to love the work of God. What began as a simple commitment by two individuals to live for God has blossomed into a legacy encompassing 101 descendants—children, grandchildren, great-grandchildren, and great-great-grandchildren who actively serve the Lord and participate in various aspects of God's work.

As I conversed with my grandparents throughout the years, they would often recount times when they could have glanced backward and considered turning around or giving up. Life wasn't always easy and pleasant; the road they traversed was sometimes lined with trials and tribulations. Yet their determination to follow the path the Lord laid before them prevailed, and the results speak for themselves. My grandfather frequently shared this wisdom: "It is hard to live for God easy, but it is easy if you live for God hard!"

In keeping with the values instilled in my family for four generations on both my father's and mother's side, it is not merely about resisting the temptation to look back but also about embracing the pursuit and passion to keep moving forward. It goes beyond the present moment and includes the formation of a lasting legacy. The focus isn't just on thinking bigger but on thinking long-term. What can I build that serves as a testament not only to me or my family but to generations yet to come? What can I initiate today that will withstand the test of time, guided by the understanding that we are called to make continuous progress?

A single backward glance has the potential to alter everything! One fleeting moment of weakness, one slip of the hand from the plow of commitment, and the lion will spring forth and urge you to retreat and surrender. You cannot effectively invest in the future if you are constantly fixated on the past. You must keep your eyes focused on the prize ahead!

Consider the plight of the Israelites. They had just experienced the most monumental deliverance in history. God had broken the shackles of Egyptian bondage and guided them toward a land flowing with milk and honey. Can you fathom their joy and excitement as they walked through the Red Sea on dry ground?

Unfortunately, the joy didn't last long, for the pursuit of their future collided with the reality of formidable giants and fortified cities in the Promised Land. Ten of the twelve spies Moses had sent on a reconnaissance mission returned utterly terrified by what they had witnessed in the land of Canaan. Although they brought back samples of the abundant fruit of the land and acknowledged that it indeed matched God's description, there was an ominous "nevertheless." Listen to the description given by ten of the twelve spies:

> Now they ... came back to Moses and Aaron and all the congregation of the children of Israel in the Wilderness of Paran, at Kadesh; they brought back word to them and to all the congregation, and showed them the fruit of the land. Then they told him, and said: "We went to the land where you sent us. It truly flows with milk and honey, and this is its fruit. Nevertheless the people who dwell in the land are strong; the cities are fortified and very large; moreover we saw the descendants of Anak there. The Amalekites dwell in the land of the South; the Hittites, the Jebusites, and the Amorites dwell in the mountains; and the Canaanites dwell by the sea and along the banks of the Jordan." (Numbers 13:26–29)

This negative report led to a distressing consequence: the people of God endured forty years of wandering in the wilderness. A single moment of fear sparked instant complaining and grumbling among the congregation. Rather than progressing forward, the Israelites contemplated a retreat; they looked back at their past and desired to return to Egypt. Worst of all, their lack of faith in pursuing and moving toward the land God had promised to them led to the death of an entire generation. When we choose not to contend for our future and instead yearn for a return to our origins, the consequences will impact both our own lives and the lives of our family members.

Several years ago, I did a study on the challenges faced by the Israelites due to their failure to invade the Promised Land.

THE LION OF LOOKING BACK

I identified several behaviors that impacted not just the ones who made that choice but future generations as well.

1. They lacked faith in God's plan, doubting that where He was leading them could be better than where they were.

2. They yearned for the past when confronted with difficulties, perceiving it as a simpler path.

3. They shifted blame onto their leaders when times grew tough and they didn't get their way.

4. They accentuated what they saw as shortcomings in their leaders.

5. When circumstances turned grim, they fixated on the negative aspects of everything.

6. They disregarded God's Word, deeming His requirements too burdensome.

7. They mistakenly believed that stepping into the Promised Land would be effortless.

8. They openly expressed discontent to those in charge and were often dissatisfied.

9. They lacked the courage to champion God's path when others were grumbling.

10. They placed greater importance on the familiar than on the future.

THE LION OF LOOKING BACK

11. They prioritized earthly comforts over heavenly promises.

These are just a few of the challenges that emerged when God's people hesitated to move forward and embrace all the promises God had prepared for them. When I say we must vigorously pursue the promises that lie ahead, I'm not suggesting it will be a walk in the park. Undoubtedly, challenges will arise. However, the rewards awaiting us in the future will far surpass anything we've left behind in the past.

Despite Joshua and Caleb's impassioned pleas to the people, reminding them of God's presence and their ability to conquer the land, the lion of looking back had inflicted a grievous wound on their faith. The poison of this temptation spread like wildfire throughout the camp, ensnaring everyone except Moses, Aaron, Joshua, and Caleb.

I've frequently considered what drove these chosen children of God to look back and yearn for a return to the bondage of Egypt. What thoughts occupied their minds as they contrasted the beauty of God's divine promise to the ugliness of their former slavery? These were the sons and daughters appointed by God, emancipated from Pharaoh's cruel taskmasters and promised a land of abundance. Yet they clung to the remnants of their slave mentality. It's disheartening when sons and daughters adopt the behaviors and mindset of captivity!

The probable cause of people looking back may be that they lack an adequate understanding of the identity God has prepared for them. God has so much in store for His children, yet we are often afraid of stepping into it because of the challenges it presents.

I'm concerned that we often find ourselves caught between two crucial "crossings" in life. The initial crossing is signified by the deliverance experienced by God's children when they left Egypt. Our salvation is depicted by the parting of the Red Sea and the destruction of Pharaoh's army. However, God envisions a subsequent crossing for His people—the crossing of possession, which seems to pose a greater challenge for us. It involves crossing the Jordan River and fighting to obtain the promises God has in store. Regrettably, when the spies returned with a negative report, those who had been delivered from Egypt failed to embark on this second crossing. Instead, they chose to dwell on the past rather than advance toward the future.

Celebrating our deliverance by mirroring Miriam's jubilant tambourine dance on Israel's day of liberation is indeed uplifting, but it should not end there. We must also possess the determination to forge ahead into the adversary's territory and claim the promises that await us.

Too often we choose to prolong the celebration of our freedom from bondage while neglecting to recognize that God led us out of Egypt with the intention of leading us into the Land of Promise. Our purpose extends beyond merely rejoicing in our freedom; we are commissioned to progress toward the fullness of what God has planned for our lives. We are not meant to remain stuck in a wilderness journey, nor are we meant to gaze backward at the place of our former bondage.

Giving up and retreating are easier than placing faith in the promise. While the promise may have been spoken, it is crucial to understand that effort is required to attain it. Regrettably, an entire generation never witnessed God's promise for their future. They perished in the wilderness during their forty-year trek through the desert.

Jesus alluded to another example of looking back when He uttered a brief but impactful three-word sermon:

THE LION OF LOOKING BACK

"Remember Lot's wife!" We are not told this woman's name, age, hair color, Enneagram number, or DISC profile; she is simply known as Lot's wife, who cast a lingering glance backward despite being explicitly instructed not to do so. God was guiding Lot's family away from the impending destruction of Sodom and Gomorrah. On this hasty departure, the primary directive was clear: they were not to cast a backward glance. Nevertheless, whatever lay behind Lot's wife seemed more significant to her than what lay ahead. In one fateful instant she looked back—and in the next instant she was turned into a pillar of salt.  *Giving up and retreating are easier than placing faith in the promise.* We shouldn't fixate on the past, regardless of how nostalgic—or conflicted—our perception may be. Living in the realm of "what ifs" is an unproductive place to live. It can lead to stumbling, surrendering, and a sense that there's nothing worth advancing toward.

Throughout history, abundant, noteworthy examples emphasize the counsel never to look back but passionately pursue progress to reap future rewards. One example is that of Hernán Cortés. In 1519, Cortés embarked on an expedition to Mexico, driven by the ambition to conquer the land. Legend has it that upon arrival in Mexico, Cortés ordered his sailors to burn the ships, effectively severing any path of retreat. After the ships were destroyed, there was no looking back. The sailors became soldiers and helped their leader accomplish his mission.

Backing away stalls forward momentum, making it vitally important that we maintain continuous movement forward.

THE LION OF LOOKING BACK

I've encountered many individuals who paid a steep price for looking back—not just for themselves but for those coming after them as well. The Bible tells us that the Lord orders the steps of a righteous person. Although your steps may be divinely ordered, they still require effort and action. If you don't take those essential steps, the Lord's guidance becomes irrelevant and useless. You must keep stepping! Progress can be achieved only when you are determined to overcome the barriers that are blocking your way.

The words of Jesus continue to ring loud and clear: "No one, having put his hand to the plow, and looking back, is fit for the kingdom of God" (Luke 9:62). I challenge you to do as the apostle Paul suggested. "Brethren, I do not count myself to have apprehended; but one thing I do, forgetting those things which are behind and reaching forward to those things which are ahead, I press toward the goal for the prize of the upward call of God in Christ Jesus" (Philippians 3:13–14).

Paul also reminded the Galatians, "Now that you have come to know God, or rather to be known by God, how can you turn back again to the weak and worthless elementary principles of the world, whose slaves you want to be once more?" (Galatians 4:9, ESV). Paul exhorted the church to recall that since God knew them, they were positioned in such a way that returning to worldly pursuits would lead them back into slavery. Once God initiates a work within us, it is unwise to look back, as the repercussions can be disastrous.

I've made many mistakes and looked back in more ways than I care to count, but I'm determined in my spirit to do what Paul was telling me to do—keep looking ahead! It is not enough to do nothing but dream of a potential future. We must get up from the couches of comfort and compromise and step into the unknown where faith is activated and dreams come to fruition.

THE LION OF LOOKING BACK

Keep moving forward regardless of the seemingly insurmountable obstacles, and have faith that you will attain the ultimate purpose of Jesus Christ's call actively working in your life. This is your divine design! God has remarkable blessings awaiting you, but it is paramount that you never give in to the lion by looking back. Just as driving a car necessitates focusing on the road ahead rather than fixating on the rearview mirror, moving forward is the only way to progress.

I have faith in you and am convinced that God has remarkable blessings in store for your future. Keep pressing forward!

Study Questions

1. How can we reconcile the importance of learning from the past without dwelling on it—without "looking back" as discussed in the text? What is the right balance between reflection and forward progress?

2. The author mentions the dangers of returning to the past, even when the future holds difficult challenges. How can we apply the lessons from historical examples like the Israelites or Lot's wife to our own lives and avoid the allure of the past when faced with challenges?

3. The story of Hernán Cortés destroying his ships to eliminate the option of retreat is presented as a symbol of unwavering commitment. In what ways can we adopt a similar level of determination and commitment in our own pursuits, especially when faced with the temptation to look back and retreat from our goals?

13

THE LION
OF LIMITATIONS

True strength emerges not in the absence of limitations but through the unwavering resolve to overcome them.

As I began writing this book, I felt the presence of a lion that seemed to be slinking closer every time I sat down to write. This lion has always been with me, lurking in the shadows, ready to pounce whenever I felt uncertain or incapable.

As I mentioned before, I was born with only one hand; my left arm ends just below the elbow. This has presented me with many challenges and obstacles through the years. My intention in sharing this is not to seek sympathy but to underscore our incredible capabilities, even in moments of limitation, and to highlight how we can overcome life's challenges through faith.

As I contemplated how to put this chapter together, my thoughts went back to numerous instances where the lion of limitations tried to drag me into an abyss of fear, doubt, and frustration. I owe a debt of gratitude to my parents, Harold and Judy Sargent, who helped me confront this adversary during my formative years. I can't express enough how often they descended into the pit, much like Benaiah, all the while reminding me of the wisdom found in the Word of God, written by the apostle Paul: "I can do all things through Christ who strengthens me" (Philippians 4:13).

You can do a lot with a *can!*

My physical appearance raised concerns not only for my parents but also for the medical professionals attending my birth. In fact, immediately after my arrival, the doctor informed my parents of potential health issues they needed to investigate to ensure my well-being. Thankfully, the only two issues I had were that I was very handsome and I was missing my left hand! I won't go into the issue with my ears. Let's just say there's a possibility that Disney might have drawn inspiration from them when creating Dumbo, the flying elephant.

I'm sure that raising a child whom many considered disabled was difficult for my parents. They have shared many moments with me from my childhood that caused them to dig in their heels and defeat the lies that tried to convince them I would never succeed. One account that never fails to move me is a story from the weeks following my birth. My dad's sister, Linda, came to see my parents. She was holding me when my father turned to her and said, "Don't worry, Linda. There won't be anything my son cannot do."

Such was the approach and attitude my parents practiced and instilled in me during my formative years. Before Nike ever coined the phrase "Just Do It," my parents were already speaking it and living it.

I recall the day I learned how to ride a bicycle. If you were the son of Harold Sargent, training wheels were not part of the equation. On my fifth birthday, I was given an Evel Knievel bike. I vividly remember my mother being worried when I climbed onto the bicycle, and understandably so—she was concerned because I was a little short-handed. However, my father had a different mindset; he simply gave

THE LION OF LIMITATIONS

me a gentle push and waited to see what would unfold. What many deemed impossible became a reality that day as I began to pedal and never looked back. Perhaps it was the allure of the Evel Knievel bike with its fake gas tank, or simply the fact that there was no other option in my parents' eyes.

I acknowledge that riding a bicycle may seem like a simple task, but many individuals might have viewed my condition as a limitation, preventing me from embarking on adventurous journeys. I'm grateful my parents firmly believed my limitations wouldn't hinder my progress.

You may not possess a physical disability like some assume I have, but there is a lurking lion of limitations that threatens to pounce on you if you permit it, potentially obstructing your path toward your rightful destiny. Perhaps this lion has frequently infiltrated your thoughts, persuading you that you'll never achieve your goals. This phenomenon originates from your brain's instinct to shield you from the discomfort you have experienced from past failures or rejections.

God can take what you might consider a limitation and transform it.

Nothing is impossible with God! God can take what you might consider a limitation and transform it into a valuable lesson that will bless everyone you encounter. Almighty God has the power to reverse any situation and bring His plans for your life to fruition, but you must battle this lion until it ceases to exist.

It is essential to understand the seriousness of believing in limitations. These harmful thought patterns can be deeply rooted and significantly influence your mindset, actions, and

THE LION OF LIMITATIONS

choices, hindering you from achieving your full potential. Belief in limitations can pertain to you, other people, or the world around you. These beliefs act as mental obstacles that obstruct personal development and success.

How frequently have you permitted this adversary to constrain you, not solely through the challenges you encounter but also through the mistaken beliefs you've accumulated throughout your life's journey? Growing up, there were many who attempted to convince me that I couldn't achieve certain things, and if I had heeded their words, you might not be reading this book today.

Throughout my life, there have been moments when others dismissed me due to what they saw as a limitation. This would ignite a fire within me, propelling me beyond their judgments and preconceptions about who I was based solely on my birth circumstances.

I reject the notion of living according to someone else's presumptions about who I am or who I can become with the help of God. Life is brief and eternity is long, so it's important not to passively abide by the expectations of others. I hope this same passion inspires you to break free from the limitations imposed by others or by past personal failures.

Allow me to share another personal example. When I was nineteen, I was in a relationship with a lady who was three or four years older than I. We had been dating for some time and had started discussing a potential future together. As our relationship progressed, I noticed her increasingly condescending attitude. One day while we were on a date, she said to me, "You're a freak of society. People look at you strangely when we enter a place of business." I wanted to fire back that it was because of my dashing looks, but I held my peace. She continued, "I'm not certain I could marry you because someone I might want to know what it feels like to be held by a man with two hands."

Suffice it to say, I ended the relationship with a parting word that was a bit out of character for me but true: "I'm not the one with a handicap. You are!"

Frequently, what we perceive as constraints are a product of labels others have placed on us. If we permit these judgments to shape our identity, we risk dwelling in a realm of limitations, forever eluding the potential that awaits us. Don't let anyone put a label on you that constricts your potential and ushers limitations into your life. You possess a wealth of potential to contribute to the Kingdom, and it's time to break free from the limitations that have held you back. Shed any doubts and uncertainties that have shackled you, abandon the territory of others' opinions of your life, and step confidently into God's promises.

God's promises are timeless; they don't come with expiration dates. As the Scriptures affirm, "God, who began the good work within you, will continue his work until it is finally finished on the day when Christ Jesus returns" (Philippians 1:6, NLT). Find strength and encouragement in Paul's words that affirm your ability to achieve all things through Jesus Christ.

For another example from Scripture, consider the woman with the issue of blood. When this woman had exhausted all her money on all available remedies for her condition, she stretched out her feeble hand to touch the hem of Jesus' garment. By doing so, she experienced complete healing. This woman illustrates that Jesus is drawn to those who reach out when they've reached the end of their resources and have the faith to believe that all things are possible with God.

Limitations may not be physical in nature; they also can stem from familial, relational, or financial issues.

THE LION OF LIMITATIONS

Furthermore, some people may struggle with negative words hurled at them since childhood, creating barriers that seem impossible to overcome. These difficult situations can create limits in the minds and hearts of individuals, forcing them to struggle constantly in order to escape the confines of their circumstances.

Limitations often obstruct the path of those destined for greatness. As you read these words, you may witness the shadow of limitations emerging from the depths of your consciousness as you strive to achieve something significant in your life. Perhaps it's the call to embark on a missions trip or to craft something that aligns with your talents and innate gifts. Maybe there's a book within you waiting to be written. Could it be that God has laid a city on your heart, a place where He desires you to establish a church? Perhaps you're the first person in your family daring to pursue a college degree, and the roar of limitations is endeavoring to intimidate you from setting foot on that college campus. God has called us to accomplish so much, and we must not let the lion of limitations deter us from fulfilling everything God has placed within our hearts.

The first step in overcoming limitations is to acknowledge that our limits do not restrict God. God surpasses our weaknesses, overcomes our fears, and prevails over any falsehood the adversary may have led us to believe. I've experienced numerous moments in my life when I felt imprisoned by the constraints of limitations and had to bring my fear and frustration before God. It was during those times that I came to realize how God operates in our weakness. His greatest work often emerges when we've exhausted our own abilities and have nowhere else to turn. The apostle Paul learned that his true strength surfaced when he was at his weakest.

THE LION OF LIMITATIONS

Our God is in perpetual motion, shaping our lives and empowering us to conquer any obstacle that impedes our journey toward becoming the person He intended for us to be. The God dwelling within you surpasses any force in this world. Your destiny is one of greatness because you serve a victorious and magnificent Savior.

Break through your limitations and turn to the limitless God. Have faith in His ability to rescue you from the lion's jaws that try to drain the life out of your dreams and hopes. You are greater than the words others may have spoken about you. Your past, which may have seemed to define you, is not the true measure of your identity. You are a beloved child of God. Limits do not define your destiny!

Study Questions

1. How can personal limitations, whether physical or mental, be transformed into sources of strength and resilience, as demonstrated by the author's personal experiences?

2. In what ways do limiting beliefs and the words of others hinder individuals from realizing their full potential and achieving their life's purpose?

3. The author discusses the concept of relying on God's strength in moments of weakness and vulnerability. How can one practically apply this principle to overcome personal limitations and embrace a life of purpose and abundance?

14

THE LION OF TEMPTATION

And do not lead us into temptation, but deliver us from the evil one. (Matthew 6:13)

The lion of temptation recognizes no boundaries, respects no restraints, and follows no rhythm or protocol. Its influence penetrates palaces and pulpits, political arenas and parishes, school corridors and congressional halls alike. It waits until its victim is vulnerable, fatigued, or depleted, then it strikes.

Each of us likely knows someone who has fallen victim to temptation. And we've seen the consequences ripple like the aftermath of a stone cast into a pond. Perhaps you yourself have been ambushed by this lion during a vulnerable moment in your life and dragged away to its lair. As Scripture declares, everyone is tempted when their own desires entice them and draw them away.

I would like to examine an event in David's life that occurred long after the innocence of his years as a young shepherd had passed. The consequences of this event marred the record of David's successes as king. I believe there were two lions at work in David's life that led to this tragedy: the lion of apathy and the lion of temptation.

Kings in the ancient Middle East usually engaged in battle in the spring of the year, when good weather assured there would be food along the way for the military. But this particular year, David decided to stay home. The narrative in II Samuel 11 characterizes this phase of the king's narrative with the following statement: "David sent Joab and his servants with him, and all Israel; and they destroyed the people of Ammon and besieged Rabbah. But David remained at Jerusalem" (II Samuel 11:1).

Why was David derelict in his role on the battlefield? What was he thinking? We have no way of knowing, but one thing is evident: this singular action set off a chain of catastrophic consequences in David's life, the repercussions of which resonated for generations to come.

David had reached the pinnacle of success. He wore the crown with pride and excelled in every arena. His army was so skilled that he no longer needed to lead them personally into battle. His trusted men had taken on leadership roles, allowing David to govern from his throne.

It was a time of great success and abundance. Prosperity was evident everywhere. Even more impressive was the magnanimous gesture of the foreign monarch who sent timber for the construction of David's palace. It was a testament to the success and prosperity of the kingdom during this period.

Nevertheless, during the season when kings traditionally led their armies into battle, David remained at home. One evening while reclining on his bed, David climbed to the rooftop of the palace to catch the cool evening breezes. Observing the panorama of his magnificent city and the splendor of his kingdom, his gaze happened on the sight of Bathsheba bathing in the courtyard of her home. This single glance set off shockwaves that rippled throughout the kingdom, exacting from David a price far greater than he could have ever envisioned he would have to pay. In one moment,

THE LION OF TEMPTATION

the lure of temptation, like a prowling lion, pounced on the king.

The Bible states, "But each one is tempted when he is drawn away by his own desires and enticed. Then, when desire has conceived, it gives birth to sin; and sin, when it is full-grown, brings forth death" (James 1:14–15).

David's failures were just beginning. After he found out Bathsheba was pregnant with his child, David tried to conceal his actions by bringing Uriah, Bathsheba's husband, back from the battlefield to spend a few nights with his wife. To David's consternation, Uriah remained loyal to his fellow soldiers who were still on the battlefield and declined to go home to his spouse. Instead, he slept on the palace steps with David's household staff.

When Uriah eventually met his demise on the battlefield, the result of an assassination plot that David had set into motion, David summoned Bathsheba to the palace to become his wife. And within just a few months, Nathan appeared before David and told a parable about a man who wrongfully took another man's cherished lamb. This narrative aroused the king's anger, leading him to insist on retribution for the parable's protagonist. Without hesitation, Nathan thundered back at David, "You are that man! You're the one who has committed this act, and God is deeply displeased." These are the consequences Nathan prophesied would be visited on David and his household:

> "Now therefore, the sword shall never depart from your house, because you have despised Me, and have taken the wife of Uriah the Hittite to be your wife." Thus says the LORD: "Behold, I will raise up adversity against you from your own house; and I will take your wives before your eyes

and give them to your neighbor, and he shall lie with your wives in the sight of this sun. For you did it secretly, but I will do this thing before all Israel, before the sun." (II Samuel 12:10–12)

The aftermath of King David's actions had far-reaching repercussions both within his own household and throughout the kingdom.

This is the danger of the lion of temptation that often appears during unexpected seasons. We need to be vigilant and fight against this beast, just as Jesus did when He was tempted by the devil in the wilderness.

It is crucial to recognize that the three temptations Jesus encountered parallel the temptations common to humankind. The Bible describes these as the lust of the flesh, the lust of the eyes, and the pride of life—the three primary arenas in which temptation seeks to overwhelm us. Jesus' victory is a powerful reminder that we, too, can overcome these temptations by submitting to the power of the Holy Spirit.

We can prevail by arming ourselves with a deeper understanding of what they entail.

The Lust of the Flesh

Our flesh is a constant foe we must defeat daily. While we may prefer to attribute everything to external factors, or to say, "The devil made me do it," the reality is we often stray due to our own wants and impulses. To state it plainly, our fleshly desires will quickly lead us into trouble if we aren't careful.

The flesh consists of the realms of sensation: feeling, touching, tasting, smelling, hearing, and seeing. Our senses serve as the focal point of desires and impulses. The Scripture speaks to us of the dangers of our flesh. We are called to live lives governed by the Spirit of God, not by the sensual strongholds of our flesh. Just before His crucifixion, Jesus urged His disciples to remain vigilant against temptation due to the weakness of human flesh. The initial temptation faced by Jesus underscores the importance of conquering the lust of the flesh. When the devil enticed Jesus by suggesting He turn stones into bread, he was targeting Jesus' fleshly desire. Our flesh will control every aspect of our lives if we will allow it. This is why the apostle Paul advised us to crucify our flesh, putting to death its unbridled cravings—and that we need to do this daily!

If Jesus and the apostle Paul encouraged us to defeat the lust of the flesh, then we must be constantly on guard, doing our best to defeat this foe at every turn. Our flesh is sinful, and only by the grace and mercy of Jesus Christ can we overcome it.

The Lust of the Eyes

It has often been stated that our eyes are the gateway to our souls. What enters through this gateway finds its way into our hearts, emphasizing the need for caution in what we allow our eyes to behold. In His Sermon on the Mount, Jesus made a profound observation that challenged the prevailing religious norms of His era. While the Law referred primarily to acts of sin, Jesus' perspective was strikingly different.

Throughout Matthew 5, Jesus repeated a speech pattern five times: "You have heard it said . . . but I say" (paraphrased). We might say that Jesus was "raising the bar" on people's concept of sin. He emphasized the point that sin involves more nuances than we might have imagined. For example, Jesus addressed the sin of adultery:

> You have heard that it was said to those of old, "You shall not commit adultery." But I say to you that whoever looks at a woman to lust for her has already committed adultery with her in his heart." (Matthew 5:27–28)

I believe Jesus aimed to set a higher standard by emphasizing, "You may believe it's solely about the act of adultery, but I want you to understand that even a gaze fueled by lust in your heart amounts to committing the sin of adultery."

Jesus' radical statements made the self-righteous listeners uncomfortable. He boiled sin down to a heart issue. These sins come from within, from our inborn carnal nature. Sin is not simply an act; it starts with an idea conceived in the inner world, and if it isn't dealt with, it will grow and eventually give birth to acts of sin that destroy lives and families.

Sadly, we have witnessed this phenomenon time and again. The issues of our inner world have the power to mold the framework of our external world. Hence, it is essential that we consistently ensure that our inner world is guided by God and His Word. We must destroy the lions that lurk in our heart.

The Pride of Life

Pride has caused many a downfall throughout history. In a biblical sense, "the pride of life" refers to the materialistic and worldly aspects of human existence that may divert people from a spiritual or purposeful path. This includes arrogance, the pursuit of personal success and status, and an excessive emphasis on wealth, possessions, and self-importance.

The root cause of the devil's banishment from Heaven is believed to have been pride. In Isaiah 14, Satan's revolt against God is described in his five "I will" statements in which he attempted to challenge God's power. The five statements listed below are commonly interpreted as indications of pride, haughtiness, and disobedience, as Lucifer aimed to elevate himself above God and establish his own rule.

1. "I will ascend into Heaven."

2. "I will exalt my throne above the stars of God."

3. "I will sit also upon the mount of the congregation, in the sides of the north."

4. "I will ascend above the heights of the clouds."

5. "I will be like the Most High."

In each of these statements, one can discern the underlying element of pride. Lucifer, despite being no match for the supreme authority of God, believed he could overthrow God's rule and attain godlike status. Pride always lurks close to the boundary of reality, deluding its victims into believing it can transform itself into something it was never meant to be.

Pride can drive people to attempt reckless and ill-advised actions they normally would not consider. Pride convinces people they are entitled to fulfill every desire their heart imagines. It fosters the belief that they stand above divine laws and merit certain pleasures that lie outside of God's purpose for their life.

I am no longer a young man, and I cannot yet claim to be an elder. But I see a worrisome trend within the church today in which some individuals perceive themselves as the sole conveyors of God's message to this generation. I would like to caution those who believe that the more they emphasize themselves, their revival, or their self-perceived divine revelations, the more acclaim and recognition they will receive.

If we aren't cautious, social media has the potential to harm us. I'm troubled by the content I see in which some people present a distorted image of themselves. Our identity should not hinge on the "likes" or "hearts" we receive while showcasing what we want others to see as God at work through us. We deceive ourselves when we believe that our worth and value are determined by the level of support we receive on our social media posts. While God's path may not always appear glamorous, it is undeniably powerful, as it fashions us into the individuals we were uniquely created to be rather than someone else's vision of what our life should resemble.

In Acts 8 we read about the citywide revival in Samaria and the conversion of Simon the Sorcerer. The apostle Peter's reaction to this individual is worthy of note:

> And when Simon saw that through the laying on of the apostles' hands the Holy Spirit was given, he offered them money, saying, "Give me this power also, that anyone on whom I lay hands may receive the Holy Spirit." But Peter said to him, "Your money perish with you, because you thought that the gift of God could be purchased with money! You have neither part nor portion in this matter, for your heart is not right in the sight of God." (Acts 8:18–21)

Ultimately, it all boils down to our motives. A craving for the approval of others can ensnare us; once we start down that road, the outcome can be catastrophic. It leads to evaluating everything we do based on the crowd's response rather than on alignment with God's purpose. This can lead us to live a life of hypocrisy instead of one guided by God's Word and the direction of His Spirit.

As James reminds us, the cure for pride is humility:

> Therefore submit to God. Resist the devil and he will flee from you. Draw near to God and He will draw near to you. Cleanse your hands, you sinners; and purify your hearts, you double-minded. Lament and mourn and weep! Let your laughter be turned to mourning and your joy to gloom. Humble yourselves in the sight of the Lord, and He will lift you up. (James 4:7–10)

Being humble is essential to being lifted up by God. No matter how slick one's personal marketing campaign is, elevation doesn't come by self-promotion. He has pledged to bestow grace upon the humble while opposing the proud. Personally, I find myself in daily need of that grace, which empowers and inspires me to carry out God's will. Without it, the temptation to step in the corrosive trap of pride becomes easier, tainting every achievement in life with its poison.

Regardless of how powerful the urge may be to act according to your desires or the validation of others, always remember that your worth originates from God. Stay humble and watch God elevate you in His time.

Study Questions

1. How does the author highlight the insidious nature of the "lion of temptation" and its ability to strike during vulnerable moments, potentially leading individuals to make destructive choices?

THE LION OF TEMPTATION

2. In the context of David's story, how did the lion of temptation manifest itself, and what can we learn from his actions and consequences when he yielded to this temptation?

3. This chapter discusses the three primary areas of temptation: the lust of the flesh, the lust of the eyes, and the pride of life. How does the text emphasize the importance of recognizing and resisting temptation in these areas, and what strategies are suggested to overcome these temptations?

15

THE LION OF IMPATIENCE

The reason most people fail instead of succeed is they trade what they want most for what they want at the moment.
— Napoleon Bonaparte

Christmas was always a special time in the Sargent household. My brothers and I would circle everything we wanted for Christmas in the Sears & Roebuck and JCPenney catalogs. The catalogs would then be placed on the kitchen table, left open, just in case Mom and Dad needed a little hint about our holiday wishes.

One of our cherished holiday traditions was unwrapping our presents on Christmas Eve because, as everyone knows, that's when the wise men presented their gifts to baby Jesus under the starry night sky! Why wait for Christmas morning? We had a biblical example guiding us, after all. As for our stockings, they were reserved for Christmas morning, just as the ancient patriarchs advised.

It is safe to say that our youthful impatience played a role in our parents not waiting until Christmas morning to let us tear into the presents. Perhaps it was the endless stream of questions about how much longer until Christmas or the ritualistic checking off the dates on the calendar hanging on the refrigerator door. We're not entirely sure why this tradition became a staple of our Christmas holidays, but as kids, we weren't about to complain. We just hoped everything we had carefully circled in those catalogs would magically appear under the tree. Those days leading up to Christmas Eve were filled with boundless excitement as we eagerly counted the days until we could open our presents.

My wife's family adhered to the nonbiblical tradition of waiting until Christmas morning. I know—it is hard to believe the heresy! However, when we got married, I took a stand, and when we had our children, guess when we celebrated Christmas? You guessed it . . . Christmas morning!

While I playfully jest about these holiday traditions, the truth is that impatience is a foe we all grapple with, and not just in our childhood years. This impatient lion rears its head more often than we'd like to admit. It emerges when our meal isn't promptly served at our favorite local restaurant. It rises during long waits at the doctor's office or at the airport when flights are delayed. Don't let me get started on slow internet speed!

James instructed us that we are to be patient, and he reminded us where patience comes from in our lives.

> My brethren, count it all joy when you fall into various trials, knowing that the testing of your faith produces patience. But let patience have its perfect work, that you may be perfect and complete, lacking nothing. (James 1:2–4)

Did you catch that? When our faith is tested, patience is produced. If we're honest, we will admit we don't like to be tested—and we sure don't like trials. Peter also described the need for patience to be added into our lives so that we can be fruitful in the knowledge of Jesus Christ. (See II Peter 1:5–8, KJV.)

THE LION OF IMPATIENCE

Our patience can wear thin when life throws unexpected challenges our way, especially the challenges we thought we had moved past. Impatience also rears its head when someone seems to leap ahead of us in life's journey, claiming achievements we believed were rightfully ours. Regardless of the circumstances, impatience is a deadly adversary, one we should not underestimate, for it has the power to shatter promises.

Do you need some convincing? Let's take a look at the lives of Abram and Sarai. After receiving a message from God, Abram left Ur of the Chaldees. God promised him, "I will make you a great nation; I will bless you and make your name great; and you shall be a blessing" (Genesis 12:2). Abram received additional messages from God, promising even more blessings if he continued to follow Him. However, this soon-to-be-called "father of the faithful" and his wife Sarai remained childless as they traversed the desert. With each passing year, as their joints grew creaky and their hair turned white, the promise of a child seemed less likely.

Our patience can wear thin when life throws unexpected challenges our way.

This is often an issue for us as we journey through life. The promises God has spoken to us don't unfold as swiftly as we desire; they seem to linger on the distant horizon, just out of our grasp. This tries our patience, and if we aren't careful, we can end up meddling with the promises of God. This happened in the lives of Abram and Sarai.

Time marched on until the patriarch reached the age of eighty-five, and his wife was in her mid-seventies. The couple had yet to be blessed with a child. Undoubtedly, this problem was a growing issue in their household, with accusations and blame possibly being thrown at each other.

Genesis 16 brings us to a harsh reality. Sarai was desperate to give her husband a child, and her impatience was increasing with each passing day. Age was not on her side. It was taking so long for the promise to materialize that the temptation to take matters into her own hands became irresistible. Sarai proposed a plan to her husband, suggesting he should take her Egyptian servant, Hagar, as a concubine, or second wife, a practice which was common in the ancient Near East. She suggested that perhaps this was how God had intended for them to have a child. The problem with this idea is that the promise had consistently been portrayed as coming directly through Sarai. Her belief that she wasn't necessarily included in this promise could have been influenced by her age and ongoing inability to conceive, leading her to think that Abram would be the one to fulfill it. After all, God had spoken the promise to him, not her.

Unfortunately, the consequences of taking matters into our own hands are often disastrous. When we believe we can expedite God's promises by seeking shortcuts, we must exercise caution, for appearances can be deceiving. In the words of author Janette Oke, "Impatience can cause wise people to do foolish things." The decision made by Abram and Sarai to have a child through Sarai's maidservant Hagar caused significant disruption in their lives and created more problems than perhaps any other decision made in human history.

After Ishmael was born, we witness the swift unraveling of destiny stemming from this single decision. Hagar's fertility compared to Sarai's barrenness gave Hagar reason to regard her mistress with contempt. Blaming Abram for this tragic turn of events, Sarai began treating Hagar so harshly that the Egyptian maidservant fled from the camp. However, God saw Hagar's distress and instructed her to return to Sarai and submit to her. God assured Hagar that He would make a great nation out of her son, Ishmael.

God reassured Abram and Sarai, affirming that the promise was indeed on its way. He changed their names to Abraham and Sarah, highlighting a profound meaning behind their new names. But although the promise remained in force, the waiting period persisted.

It wasn't until Abraham became a centenarian and Sarah was ninety that the awaited day finally arrived, and Isaac was born. As he grew older, Sarah began to observe signs of animosity that Hagar held toward her and the promised heir. Oblivious to the family dynamic, Abraham thought everything was all right until Sarah's patience came to an end. She once again demanded that Abraham banish Hagar and Ishmael from the camp. Sarah feared that her promised son had competition, and if Ishmael should continue to be a part of the family, it could potentially hinder things from going in Isaac's favor. Sarah adamantly refused to entertain the notion of sharing the promise with Hagar's son. In her eyes, Isaac was the promised child, and she was determined not to allow the son of her Egyptian maidservant to be regarded on the same level as Isaac.

The story merits much more discussion than we can devote to it, but it underscores the point that impatience is a treacherous beast that seeks to rush things beyond the pace that aligns with God's intentions for us. We find ourselves shaping circumstances according to our own desires because of a craving for immediate gratification.

Perhaps life is more about embracing a slower pace and recognizing that God has a plan in which all things come together for our benefit. God, in His perfect timing, raises one person above another. He opens the doors He wants us to enter. We should not to let our political or social ambitions drive us to push too forcefully for what we believe is rightfully ours. Trying to force open a locked door can lead to destruction. Many individuals have been derailed by hasty choices they believed would accelerate their position or influence.

As previously mentioned, the consequence of Abraham and Sarah's impulsive decision spawned a legacy of enmity that endures to this present day. Let us earnestly seek God and confront the lion of impatience, removing it from the terrain of our lives so that it does not unleash devastation with lasting repercussions on generations to come.

Study Questions

1. How does impatience, as described in the story of Abram and Sarai, often lead to hasty decisions and unintended consequences in our own lives?

2. The author mentions that impatience is a treacherous beast that seeks to rush things beyond the pace that aligns with God's intentions for us. How can we learn to embrace a slower pace in our own lives and trust in God's timing, even when faced with challenging circumstances or unfulfilled promises?

3. Reflect on the idea that impatience can have repercussions that resonate for generations. Can you think of examples from your own life or history where impatience led to long-lasting negative consequences? How might recognizing and confronting the "lion of impatience" help us make wiser decisions and avoid such outcomes?

16

THE LION OF DECEPTION

The heart is deceitful above all things, and desperately wicked; who can know it? (Jeremiah 17:9)

Deception preys upon anyone willing to lend an ear to its lies. It is a sly and cunning creature that convinces those under its spell that God is holding out on them.

This predator set its hungry gaze upon the pinnacle of God's creation in the Garden of Eden. Upon hearing the voice of the serpent, Eve succumbed to the voice, plucked the fruit from the Tree of Knowledge of Good and Evil, and consumed it. She then offered it to her husband, Adam, who likewise partook. The consequence was utter devastation as humanity was thrust into the abyss of a fallen world, a far cry from the divine plan God had envisioned for Adam and Eve.

An examination of Jesus' words in John 8 is essential to grasp the consequences of deceit. During a conversation with religious leaders of His time, Jesus explained the devil's motives. He didn't hold back; He let the religious leaders have it, telling them they were of their "father the devil" (John 8:44). Jesus' outspoken response solidified their desire to get rid of this so-called Messiah.

By identifying them as being from the devil, Jesus established an important truth concerning the nature of Satan and his deceptive tactics. From the beginning, Satan bore the mark of a liar and a murderer. His deceit extended beyond mere falsehood; it was a sinister ploy aimed at orchestrating Adam and Eve's demise. God had told them, "In the day you eat of this tree, you will die." Satan contradicted this with the false claim, "You will not die." This deception led Jesus to denounce him as a liar and a murderer from the beginning.

It is evident that Satan knew full well the truth of God's statement because he assured the two innocents they would not face death if they consumed the fruit from the forbidden tree. Tragically, they fell for this deceit, and their actions introduced sin into the world. Thus, since the beginning, Satan has pursued a malevolent agenda to kill, steal, and destroy. His masterful trickery—built on falsehoods, incomplete information, assumptions, and misleading statements—has continued to deceive people ever since.

That pivotal moment of deception in the Garden plunged humanity into the depths of sin; however, God foretold to Adam and Eve that a day would come when someone would arise to obliterate the deeds of the devil.

The primary aim of deception is to remove humanity from their rightful position as children of God. If the adversary can seize our authority and identity, he can establish a stronghold that can be dismantled only through the precious blood of Jesus Christ. Thus, fully comprehending your identity in Christ is essential for your future as a child of God. You cannot effectively confront the challenges that arise in your life's journey if you are uncertain about your identity and the calling God has placed upon you. Without this understanding, you may struggle in your faith and become susceptible to the deceptive voice of the enemy as he tries to convince you that you lack the strength to overcome and succeed.

THE LION OF DECEPTION

The voice of deceit is prevalent today. Paul, in his letter to his young disciple Timothy, issued a warning about this, stating, "Now the Spirit expressly says that in latter times some will depart from the faith, giving heed to deceiving spirits and doctrines of demons" (I Timothy 4:1).

Essentially, the apostle was indicating that in these final days, there will be individuals who willingly surrender their minds to misleading spirits that seek to lead them astray. Satan's age-old strategies remain unchanged; he continues to employ these tactics in his efforts to divert us from the path we are called to follow.

To illustrate my perspective on the devastation of deception, I'd like to focus on one of its most insidious means: the influence of assumptions. It seems the adversary understands that all he has to do is entice us to contemplate his propositions, and in many cases the enticement starts us on the journey toward making incorrect or foolish assumptions.

The enemy's initial step toward deception involves tricking us into accepting his falsehoods as truth, leading us to assume things that have no connection to reality. Contemplate this scenario with me: What if Benaiah had interpreted the lion's descent into the pit on that momentous day as a stroke of luck? What if he had assumed the lion's disappearance meant it posed no further harm that day? Out of sight, out of danger for everyone. By assuming the lion was no longer a concern, he would have inadvertently left a potential threat for someone else to encounter, and his assumption might have resulted in a fatality. That lion would have been a menace to himself or anyone else who traversed that path in the days or weeks to come.

Failure to exercise caution in this area can lead to tragic consequences. A classic example of this is found in the life of Joseph. Joseph's brothers, driven by jealousy and enmity,

THE LION OF DECEPTION

cast him into a pit. The brothers initially intended to kill Joseph, but Reuben intervened. They were eating a meal (perhaps while ignoring Joseph's cries for help) when they heard the approach of a company of Ishmaelites bound for Egypt. Judah suggested they could sell their kid brother to the Ishmaelites, which they did for twenty shekels of silver. They then devised a ruse to conceal their horrible deed. They seized Joseph's prized coat of many colors, a garment that signified his favored status, and immersed it in the blood of a slaughtered goat.

> Then they sent the tunic of many colors, and they brought it to their father and said, "We have found this. Do you know whether it is your son's tunic or not?" (Genesis 37:31–32)

Notice the subtlety of their inquiry when they presented the coat to their father without actually stating it was Joseph's coat. Jacob immediately recognized the coat as the one he had given to his beloved son. No doubt a tourniquet of fear tightened around the heart of the elderly patriarch as he said, "It is my son's tunic. A wild beast has devoured him. Without doubt Joseph is torn to pieces" (Genesis 37:33).

Jacob assumed that a wild beast had killed his son. This patriarch's fear at this moment was nothing but *false evidence appearing real*, and it caused him years of sorrow and grief.

This is the essence of deception. The enemy presents something that has no basis in reality; he parades it in front of you like it is a solid fact, letting you draw false conclusions. You assume you do not have what it takes because of the lies he has told. You assume you will never amount to much because of your family background and the history of failure that seems to be repeated in your life. The adversary employs falsehoods to present deceptive evidence that appears convincingly real. Listening to that voice can lead you into a life filled with assumptions, hindering you from moving beyond the lie.

For how many weeks, months, or years did Jacob retreat into the depths of his heart where assumptions had fatally wounded his dreams for his beloved son Joseph? How frequently did he retrieve that blood-stained coat from the closet, shedding tears over the unrealized potential of a divine promise?

This is the aftermath of deception. It leaves you thinking things are much different than the current reality and that the future is dark and uncertain. It causes you to withdraw from others and slide into pits of doubt and fear, uncertain about your tomorrow and unwilling to advance beyond the lies you've been told.

When reflecting on the account of Adam and Eve in the Garden of Eden, we observe a consequence of deceit: once one embraces a falsehood, shame inevitably takes hold. Adam and Eve exemplified this inclination toward deception by concealing themselves from God within the Garden, burdened with shame about their nakedness and their disobedience. Deception proves to be a sinister adversary as it pulls us from our rightful place in God and causes us to shrink back from the relationship we were created to have with our Creator.

The power of deception should never be underestimated, for it has thwarted the potential of countless people and prevented them from fulfilling their true calling. By examining these biblical stories, we can grasp the urgency of defeating this beast before it takes hold and undermines our potential.

How can we defend ourselves against this mighty adversary of deception? The Word of God consistently calls for us to stand firm and resist the devil's deceitful lies that might divert us from our chosen path. Remain rooted in the truth—the Word of God. Wield His Word as a mighty sword to vanquish the lies and falsehoods propagated by the adversary. This is what Jesus did when He was tempted by Satan in the wilderness, and it is something we should do as well. Let the Word of God become deeply rooted in your spirit and defeat the lion of deception with the truth.

Study Questions

1. This chapter discusses the role of deception in leading individuals astray, using biblical examples such as Eve and Adam in the Garden of Eden. Can you think of a personal experience when you or someone you know fell victim to deception? What was the impact, and how did it affect your life and sense of purpose?

2. Deception often involves making assumptions based on false evidence that appears real. How can individuals safeguard themselves against making assumptions that lead to deception, and what role can discernment play in this process?

3. The author emphasizes the importance of remaining rooted in the Word of God to combat deception. How has your understanding of and connection to your faith or spiritual beliefs helped you discern and resist deception in your life?

17

STOP THE MOUTHS OF LIONS

Who through faith subdued kingdoms, worked righteousness, obtained promises, stopped the mouths of lions. (Hebrews 11:33)

They stand as elite figures set apart from the rest of history. These men and women initially appear otherworldly. Bravery, might, and strength are just a few of the qualities that describe and define the individuals we encounter in Hebrews 11, God's hall of faith.

However, as you delve into their lives, you quickly realize these heroes are just as human as you and me. Their pasts were sometimes marked by embarrassment and shame. They did not come from elite backgrounds or the upper echelons of society. They were ordinary men and women. But they overcame incredible challenges through their unwavering faith.

Consider Rahab. Despite her work as a harlot in Jericho's red-light district, she agreed to shelter the Hebrew spies and consequently embraced the destiny of God's people. Although her profession may have defined her up to this point, her faith allowed her to break free from the walls that held her captive. As a result, she became part of the lineage of Jesus Christ. Her story is a testament to the power of faith and its ability to transform lives.

STOP THE MOUTHS OF LIONS

Rahab is not the only figure in the faith chapter that captures our attention. While we're familiar with the names of the patriarchs we've known since our Sunday school days, some of the characters in Hebrews 11 remain nameless, yet their faith was truly remarkable. In fact, they were so mighty that one of their notable feats was stopping the mouths of lions.

Incredible! They stopped the mouths of lions that sought to thwart their destiny, obstruct their path, and hinder them from fulfilling God's promises and purposes. Hebrews 12:1 states that we are surrounded by a great cloud of witnesses, observing our progress. They are hoping we'll carry on the work they began. (See Hebrews 11:39–12:1.) We cannot achieve this goal if we let the fear of the lions overpower us. We must silence the roars of these lions, preventing them from spreading lies and asserting that we'll never overcome the inner struggles we encounter day by day. With our faith and the resilience it provides, we have the power to conquer these adversaries, but we can't accomplish it in isolation.

The central theme of this book has been the inner challenges we must overcome in order to align with God's intended purpose for our lives. We've encountered fear and temptation, confronted the challenges posed by entitlement and apathy, and grappled with many other internal struggles we encounter daily. We've examined the lions that fuel pride, tarnish our true selves, and disrupt our alignment with God's plans for our lives. The adversary is tireless in his efforts to stir up these inner lions. He sows discord in our lives, unravels families and marriages, and entices both the young and the old to forsake the pursuit of the reward that awaits those who maintain their faithfulness.

The purpose of this writing has been to help us identify the lions that lurk within ourselves as well as the tactics of the adversary who opposes us in so many arenas. It is essential to recognize our opponent for who he really is and dismantle every snare he sets, as these traps have the capability to divert us from our path forward.

The devil is a liar, and, unfortunately, our sinful nature is inclined to follow his lead unless we put on the whole armor of God and allow the power of the Holy Ghost within us to rise and demolish every falsehood the devil tries to inject into our minds and hearts.

This challenging endeavor necessitates heeding the counsel of the apostle Peter, who advised, "Be sober, be vigilant; because your adversary the devil walks about like a roaring lion, seeking whom he may devour. Resist him, steadfast in the faith" (I Peter 5:8–9).

Let me emphasize that last phrase—*resist him*! Stand firm in your faith and resist! Victory in this struggle is possible only when we actively oppose the devil's cunning tactics. We must remain vigilant for the sake of our children, our marriages, our futures, our churches, and our extended families. Attending church sporadically won't defeat the hidden lions. Taking your Bible off the shelf a few times a month won't keep the lions at bay. Giving of your time, talent, and treasures on occasion won't confine the lions to the pit; they will emerge to bring destruction on you and your family. You must be diligent and discerning concerning the enemy's schemes.

We must follow Benaiah's example on that decisive day when he encountered the lion. We must descend into the pit to confront and combat the hidden threats that are eager to sow chaos in our lives, our families, and our destinies, regardless of the circumstances or the season of life we may be in.

No matter how strong we think we are, we cannot vanquish inner lions single-handedly. We need support from God, His Word, and the influence of others.

Satan is a master of deception, exerting every effort to persuade us that we lack the capability and privilege to emerge from the fog of our failures and fears and become the individuals God intended us to be. Satan is not just deceptive; he is the father of all falsehoods. There is no truth in anything he utters or undertakes.

Peter underscored the fact that the devil falls short of the powerful image he portrays. He may roar loudly, but it is nothing but noise. The devil endeavors to deceive people into believing he possesses qualities and abilities he does not actually possess. We need to remember that no matter how many disguises he wears, he is defeated.

No matter how strong we think we are, we cannot vanquish inner lions single-handedly.

Since his attempted coup in the heavenly realm, Satan has sought to elevate himself to God's level but has failed to do so. Instead, he remains a corrupt copycat, parading around with boastful roars, hoping that his bluster will instill enough fear in people to make them back up and surrender.

There is an intriguing play on words in Genesis 3 that carries over into the New Testament. God pronounced judgment upon Satan, saying he was cursed more than every beast of the field. He was doomed to slither on his belly and eat dust all the days of his life. God declared He would put enmity between the serpent's seed and the woman's Seed, saying that although the serpent would bruise the heel of the woman's Seed, her Seed would bruise the serpent's head.

The enemy strikes at our heels, but God will have the final say by putting the enemy under His feet. He's going to crush that serpent's head! In his letter to the church at Rome, the apostle Paul wrote,

> And the God of peace shall bruise Satan under your feet shortly. The grace of our Lord Jesus Christ be with you. Amen. (Romans 16:20, KJV)

The word *bruised* comes from a Greek word meaning to crush and destroy. God's intentions for the devil are to completely demolish his attempts at deceiving and destroying humanity, and He has accomplished that through the risen Lord and Savior Jesus Christ.

This leads us to the focal point of this chapter. Despite the devil's crafty attempts to thwart our progress and lead us into passivity regarding God's purpose for our lives, he is utterly powerless against the last lion we are going to discuss: Jesus Christ, the Lion of the tribe of Judah!

This Lion is the true lion—the ultimate victor. He has come to destroy the works of Satan and dismantle the deeds of the devil. He publicly showcased His mission two thousand years ago through the crucifixion on the cross and subsequent resurrection, thereby conquering death, Hell, and the grave.

This Lion of Judah has no limitations. He has provided victory for you and me by the precious blood He shed on Calvary. All of the lurking lions discussed in this book don't have the power to defeat the Lion of Judah. He is the King of kings and Lord of lords. The enemy may present himself as the king of the jungle, but he is nothing more than a corrupt copycat!

STOP THE MOUTHS OF LIONS

We are the children of God, and because of this relationship we can take the words of Christ who said, "Behold, I give you the authority to trample on serpents and scorpions, and over all the power of the enemy, and nothing shall by any means hurt you" (Luke 10:19).

Why should you fear when the Lion of Judah has conquered them all? Take courage and remember,

> No weapon that is formed against thee shall prosper; and every tongue that shall rise against thee in judgment thou shalt condemn. This is the heritage of the servants of the LORD, and their righteousness is of me, saith the LORD. (Isaiah 54:17, KJV)

The God you serve has never had trouble with any lion. Ask Daniel. God shut the lions' mouths when Daniel was thrown in the pit, and He can silence the beasts that are currently trying to devour your life and destiny. David could affirm that with God on his side, a lion approaching his father's sheep stood no chance of survival. Stand firm in your faith, resist the devil, and, according to the Word of God, your enemy will flee.

Have faith that the One who is working in you has a plan for you and will complete that plan if you stay grounded in the truth of the Word of God and if your faith is established in God.

The Lion of Judah stands as your protector! Your God has never tasted defeat and never will. He is the all-powerful, all-knowing, sovereign Lord and Savior. Nothing lies beyond His capabilities, and He watches over every challenge and struggle you encounter. He has pledged that you are more than a conqueror. You can stop the mouths of lions!

The devil may masquerade as a roaring lion, but the Lion of Judah is above all, and there is no limit to His power and glory. Rest assured: this Lion has conquered it all, and He has given you the authority to do the same through the mighty, matchless name of Jesus!

Study Questions

1. The author emphasizes the power of faith and the ability to metaphorically stop the mouths of lions. Can you share a personal experience when your faith significantly overcame a challenging situation or obstacle, even when it seemed insurmountable?

2. The text discusses the deceptive tactics of the adversary, often portrayed as a roaring lion. In your own life, how have you recognized or encountered the adversary's deceitful strategies? What steps have you taken to resist and overcome them?

3. This chapter presents the Lion of Judah as the ultimate victor over the adversary. How does your faith in Jesus Christ impact your ability to face challenges and struggles in life, and how does it influence your perspective on the power and authority you have to overcome obstacles and adversity?

18

A FINAL WORD

I found myself alone beneath the starry canopy, composing the conclusion of this book. Surrounded by stars and satellites illuminating the night sky, I contemplated the chapters of my life that remain unwritten. How many more years remain, and how many more doors will God graciously open for me to step through on this journey so that I may impact my family, friends, and others?

Then I thought of the words Paul wrote to Timothy, his young protégé in the gospel,

> Fight the good fight of faith, lay hold on eternal life, to which you were also called and have confessed the good confession in the presence of many witnesses. (I Timothy 6:12)

Nothing of true value enters our lives without a battle. It goes beyond merely thinking positive thoughts about what we aspire to be; it requires unwavering determination and effort to overcome the lions that have lain dormant beneath the surface for years, waiting for the opportunity to surface and disrupt our lives and legacy.

Your life holds significance, and with that significance comes the responsibility to infuse it with purpose. This

A FINAL WORD

requires standing firm against the forces that seek to dismantle the worth of your existence.

I can't assure you the path ahead will be smooth, but I can assure you that if you persist—if you courageously face the depths where fear, temptation, and other challenges lurk—you will emerge on the other side with the knowledge that your struggles provided meaning, and you will have defeated the adversary who sought to obstruct your journey.

As you read the last few words of this book, my deepest wish and prayer is that you will thrive and fully embody the person God has destined you to be. With God by your side, nothing is beyond your reach. And as you grapple with the challenges that surround you, always remember that greater is He that is inside of you than he that is in the world!

Your life has been designed to profoundly impact your generation, but this can happen only when you (1) acknowledge the battles you must confront and (2) defeat the lions that continuously emerge from the pit to impede your journey. To this, I proclaim: Keep fighting!

Fight until the sword becomes an extension of your hand.

Fight until Hell surrenders and Heaven celebrates.

Fight until the beasts that approach you tremble and flee, fearing the divine strength within you.

Fight until fear dissipates and faith overcomes the challenges in your path.

Fight until what is altered inside of you revolutionizes everything around you.

Fight until you emerge victorious against every lion that has sought to conquer you throughout your life, and keep fighting until your words become catalysts for transformation in the lives of others!

A FINAL WORD

Fight! Your marriage depends on it.
Fight! Your family is looking to you for victory.
Fight! Your children must know their future is secure in you and in God.
Fight! Your legacy is being lengthened as you wrestle with every beast that tries to overtake you!

Always keep in mind that no weapon formed against you shall prosper. You are anointed by God to be a lion-slayer, and the best is yet to come in your life. Therefore, keep fighting, trusting, moving, and believing—because great things are ahead for you!

In his speech at the Sorbonne in Paris (April 23, 1910), President Theodore Roosevelt uttered these iconic words:

> It is not the critic who counts; not the man who points out how the strong man stumbles, or where the doer of deeds could have done them better. The credit belongs to the man who is actually in the arena, whose face is marred by dust and sweat and blood; who strives valiantly; who errs, who comes short again and again, because there is no effort without error and shortcoming; but who does actually strive to do the deeds; who knows great enthusiasms, the great devotions; who spends himself in a worthy cause; who at the best knows in the end the triumph of high achievement, and who at the worst, if he fails, at least fails while daring greatly, so that his place shall never be with those cold and timid souls who neither know victory nor defeat.

A FINAL WORD

I pray this book has impacted your life as you've read through it. I may not know you personally, where you came from, or the challenges you've had to overcome, but I believe God is working in you to do His good pleasure. Your life is too valuable not to leave a lasting imprint on your family, community, and the world at large! Step out in faith, knowing that He who has begun a good work in you will complete it. That's a promise.

Get into that arena and fight those adversaries that lurk beneath the surface! Stop the mouths of those lions. There is so much in store for your life!

Keep slaying lions.

Study Questions

1. How does the metaphor of fighting lions and facing hidden obstacles resonate with your life journey and determination to become the person you were meant to be?

2. This chapter mentions that "nothing of true value enters our lives without a battle." Can you share a personal experience or challenge you've faced that reinforces this idea in your own life?

3. The author concludes with the idea of stepping into the arena with great daring. How can you apply this mindset to overcome obstacles, make a lasting impact, and fulfill your purpose in life?

Made in United States
North Haven, CT
29 July 2024